You've $\sum_{n=1}^{\infty}$ Got Algorithm

But Can You Dance?

Roberto Giannicola

You'v$\overset{\infty}{\underset{n=1}{\Sigma}}$ Got Algorithm

But Can You Dance?

Learn how to lead with heart and empathy

First Printing, 2022
Paperback ISBN 979-8-9857354-0-6
E-Book ISBN 979-8-9857354-1-3
Giannicola Inc.
www.giannicola.com
YOU'VE GOT ALGORITHM, BUT CAN YOU DANCE?™ (Trademark)

Contents

Acknowledgments..7

Workbook..9

Introduction.. 11

Part 1: Learning How to Dance 15

Chapter 1: One Cocky Coward 17

Chapter 2: What Does It Mean to "Dance"?...............33

Chapter 3: Will You Enter the Bar?...............43

Chapter 4: Grow, or Live to Regret It..................55

Chapter 5: Who Are You? 65

Chapter 6: Kintsugi Yourself 79

Chapter 7: How Your Need for Validation
Can Affect You 91

Chapter 8: Self-Sabotage and Overcoming
Your Limits 103

Part 2: Dancing with Others 115

Chapter 9: Mind Your Language........................ 117

Chapter 10: Countersteering and the Art of
Listening 129

Chapter 11: To Be as Free as Giuseppe 141

Chapter 12: They Are Fine; They Can Take It 153

Chapter 13: Stop Telling Them What to Do—
Coach Them Instead 167

Ask Meaningful Questions 179

The Coaching Framework 183

Chapter 14: How to Give Them Critical

    Feedback—the Right Way 191

Giving Constructive Feedback 194

Giving Recognition and Praise 198

Chapter 15: You Need More Empathy;

    Here Is How to Get It 201

Part 3: Creating Your Own Dance 219

Chapter 16: Off the Dance Floor and Onto

    the Balcony 221

Being in Reactive Mode 223

When Hoarding Knowledge Prevents People's

    Growth 226

What It's Like to Dance on the Balcony 229

Chapter 17: Planning Your Self-Transformation 237

Development Action Plan (DAP) 240

Motivation and Transformation Quadrant

    (MTQ) 245

Chapter 18: Stuck Between a Hammer and a

    Cappuccino 255

Chapter 19: Play It All Out 261

Appendix 265

Coaching Model Sample Conversations 265

Coaching Model Sample Questions 274

References and Resources 281

Acknowledgments

I've heard many people say that time flies when they reminisce about their past. They say things like, "Wow, I feel like I graduated, moved, got married, had a child, just yesterday." Not me. I feel like many moments in my life happened ages ago. So many experiences, places, and people have come and gone that I feel it has taken a very long time to get where I am today. Because of that, the first part of my acknowledgments and gratitude goes to these moments—the many people and the myriad experiences that have made me who I am. Whether you know it or not, whether you are a longtime friend or someone I met only briefly, whether you were fun to be with or a total pain in the ass, somehow, you have contributed to my transformation. For that, I thank you.

A very special thank-you to my dear friend Jürgen Möllers, founder of Storyzon (storyzon.com). Your gentle guidance throughout this journey was always right on point. You helped me improve every chapter. You challenged my ideas and pushed me to make this book so much better. All right, I'll admit it, I really like you, and I'm so grateful for you and our friendship.

Erik Campbell, you're a rock star editor. You got my voice and added the right fairy dust and rainbow glitter all around.

I want to thank my friend Lori Thomas for coming up with the best title for this book. You are such a fun, clever, and creative person, and I appreciate you.

Thank you to all the early reviewers of the book. You brought so much insight, and you helped me with the final changes.

To my daughter, Anna-Sofia, you've guided and shaped me in more ways than you know. You are a precious gem, and I love you so much. Thank you for helping me design the cover of this book.

Robin Treasure, you're the reason I wrote this book. You've inspired me all along, and I'm so grateful and lucky to have you in my life. I can't wait to see what's on our next pages.

Workbook

Throughout this book, I offer references to material that you can access on my website, www.giannicola.com. You can download a free workbook that will give you examples, additional questions, and templates for the points I'm addressing in this book.

Introduction

There is an old, well-known story.

A man has lost his keys. It's the middle of the night, the power is out, and the house is pitch-black. Since he can't see anything, he decides to go outside to search for his keys around the lamppost at the street corner.

His neighbor shows up, wondering what is going on.

"I lost my keys," the man tells his neighbor.

"Let me help you look," the neighbor replies.

After a short while, the neighbor asks, "Where exactly did you lose your keys?"

"Well, somewhere in my house."

"What?" the neighbor says. "Why are we searching for them out here, then?"

The man looks at the neighbor with surprise. "Because it doesn't make sense to grope around in a dark house. The light is out *here*."

This story is poignant because it captures an essential truth: when faced with a challenge, rather than looking for where the problem truly lies, we often look toward what is familiar, to a place where we can use our usual tools. This is particularly true when it comes to emotional challenges: we often prefer to retreat into our familiar self than to step into the "darkness" of the unknown.

I would know. In my early years, I spent far too much time crawling around lampposts. And today, as a leadership coach who has worked with hundreds of managers and executives of Fortune 500 companies, I see so many people similarly searching for their keys outside of their homes, believing they'll find solutions externally rather than internally. I have come to realize that there is one main difference that separates those who excel in leadership from the rest: outstanding leaders know how to navigate the social and emotional challenges of their day-to-day interactions with ease and fluidity. Such ability is not the result of greater factual knowledge or a specific set of external rules. Rather, it flows naturally from a mindset in which experience, understanding, and empathy have come into alignment. A mindset that is based on honest self-observation and made possible by a willingness to change.

One of the first things I tell my clients is that there is nothing I coach or facilitate that I have not gone through myself. Yes, I was that guy who knew how to read algorithms, develop software, and manage complex projects. And yet, interpersonally I was a big mess. Stubborn, rigid, and awkward, I was painfully poor at managing my emotions.

So I embarked on a journey of self-development. My biggest assets were curiosity and determination. I really wanted to understand what it would take to feel comfortable in socially diverse situations. I wanted to be free—or at least freer—more comfortable with myself and better attuned to others. I wanted to be able to receive input with an open mind and exert influence with grace and empathy.

My first stumbling steps of self-discovery put me onto a path that led to where I am today: helping people achieve what they desire and facilitating their self-growth. For more than ten years, I have guided industry leaders to better identify core challenges in their lives and learn ways to overcome them with confidence. Nothing motivates me more than seeing capable people take on a challenge and dare to be their true selves.

When we experience failure, we often leap headfirst into a new relationship or a new job, without taking the time to understand why we failed in the first place. Or we simply blame others. We do just about anything to stay close to our lamppost, because we think we need the external light to guide us. Without it, we think, we would be unable to see.

So many of us have learned to resolve complex problems on-screen. We write algorithms and lines of code, and tackle issues with well-designed diagrams. But when it comes to more intangible problems, like communication, personalities, and behaviors, we get lost.

If we want to get a promotion, increase our earning capacity, influence people, and become an admired leader, our technical knowledge and degrees will only get us so far. To advance further, we need a different skill set, we need self-awareness and the ability to connect with people. We need to be courageous, take a good look inside ourselves, and find our own light. In short, we need emotional intelligence.

Fortunately, we can all achieve this change; challenging as it may be at times, it is within our reach. It's like learning to dance. We hear and feel the music, we envision the steps, but we need to learn how to actually put it all into motion. To do that, we need to understand what holds us back and what limits our confidence and attitude. Then we need to listen to the beat, learn the steps, and practice them until we become fluid in our movements. Once that happens, we need to learn how to dance with a partner and lead with passion and grace. Only when we have mastered all of that can we create our own authentic dance, with charisma, style, and grace.

My own journey has not been an easy one. I have learned the hard way how much commitment, curiosity, and courage self-transformation takes. But I firmly believe that there are no viable alternatives. If you don't want to take the journey, if you continue to look for your keys around some lamppost, you may end up dying with the music still in you, as Wayne Dyer has said. But if you start by examining yourself with curiosity and compassion, I can promise you, you will be able to reach your potential and express yourself fully.

So, what do you think? Do you care to play some music and learn how to dance?

Part 1

Learning How to Dance

As experts in our respective fields, many of us have learned to believe that professional expertise and deliverables are the only things that matter. At the end of the day, we need to get the job done—isn't that what counts?

Yes, it does indeed, but how often do we find ourselves wishing we could better navigate certain social contexts, read people more accurately, and feel more relaxed and self-confident? How often do we wish we could dance, rather than stand on the sidelines?

Learning how to dance requires self-awareness and honesty. If we don't understand our emotions, what things trigger us, and how we can respond differently, we are bound to repeat the same missteps, and step on our partners' toes.

Fortunately, you can learn how to pay attention to your emotions and perceptions, as well as their effects on your environment. You can learn to recognize and acknowledge your self-worth by removing your inner saboteurs and your need for external validation. Doing so will enable you to lead and inspire people, advance your personal growth, and attain your goals.

Chapter 1

One Cocky Coward

Dancing with two left feet

Most days are like any other: unremarkable, in muted colors, and often forgotten. But from time to time, particularly if you are present enough to recognize them, you have those moments that make a particular day stand out vividly.

For me, one of these moments occurred early in my career when I was in a conference room with a group of managers and directors, discussing the development of a financial software application for a large bank in California.

I had been working there as a contractor for over six months, and the higher-ups were considering making me the primary person to develop and manage this application.

The meeting was set up to give all the stakeholders an idea of how I would build it, what analysis I would do, and what difficulties I anticipated.

I was warned that the panel would include not only my boss but also my boss's boss and the department head. Now, I was comfortable addressing one level up, but three layers of management was something I hadn't expected, and the prospect caused me no small amount of anxiety. I began to barrage myself with possibilities, most of them of a negative inclination: What if they asked me questions I didn't know the answers to? Was I good enough to manage this process? Was I a fraud? If I were a fraud, could they tell? I could feel my discomfort mounting.

My manager had called me a few days before to tell me that while we normally wore casual attire, this particular meeting probably required something a bit more formal. Now, *that* I thought was an easy one; I would wear the blue-and-yellow-checkered jacket I had brought back from my summer trip to Italy. The jacket, I knew, would emphasize how important this meeting was to me. And, like me, the jacket was Italian-fancy and emblematic of style and readiness.

Now I felt more prepared.

The big day came. I was a bit nervous but felt ready for the challenge.

I made a point of leaving the house early. San Francisco traffic can be unpredictable, and the city bus system was no different. I boarded, showed the driver my pass, and walked the center aisle toward the back. I got some looks and smiles from the passengers who normally saw me in jeans and an informal shirt. I was disappointed that the cute brunette who usually sat in the third row was not there that day. I know she could have offered me a dose of comfort. She might have even thought I looked amazing. Devastatingly and rather mysteriously European.

I got off at my stop and walked a few blocks down Montgomery Street, the main thoroughfare of San Francisco's Financial District. By then, I felt pretty confident. In hindsight though, "cocky" might be the better word, as I strutted toward my office in my flamboyant jacket.

The meeting was scheduled for 10:00 a.m. The conference room was in the center of the floor plan—windowless, stuffy, and warm. I couldn't help but notice everyone's reactions when they saw me in that highly expressive jacket. I felt a rush of heat rising inside me. I chose a spot around the large table and sat down.

Eric, my boss, greeted me, and everyone else offered friendly smiles. As I pulled papers and plans out of my folder, my hands were moist (the papers, too, would soon be wet). Eric explained the outline of the project and then introduced everyone around the room. Then he pointed at me and said, "Roberto will now give us the plan he has in mind to develop this application."

Off I went. I laid out my design and timelines. I shared the requirements and explained who would be involved in the process. My tone was direct and to the point. I felt competent and knowledgeable. I was in charge, in control. This was going well.

When I finished presenting my perfect, airtight plan, the questions started coming in—not just a few, but a veritable assault of questions came at me. Or at least that's how it felt.

Years later I would realize that everything changed in that meeting because I felt that I was no longer in charge.

People were kind to me and curious about many aspects of the project, but back then I suspected they were doubting my competence. When they asked about specific dates, for example, I thought they were questioning my ability to deliver on time, and so, with my Italian accent and in a lamentably curt tone, I said, "Don't worry, I'll get it done."

Then I pointed out that they needed to provide me with access to their data or they would delay the project. When they asked me what I would do if access were delayed, I sat back in my chair, crossed my arms defensively, and answered with something along the lines of, "Well, *you* have to do your part of the work. I hope you won't blame *me* if the project falls behind." This was, needless to say, not the most skillful answer.

The more questions that came in, the more I felt judged, cornered, and consequently, threatened—the archetypal fight-or-flight response. Instead of validating their concerns, I forced my perspective on them—in fact, I threw it over them like a heavy, itchy blanket: "Here is what I think would be the best way to tackle problems, bring solutions, address people or situations."

I went on and on. I was barely listening, and instead of communicating with my audience, I was *telling* them what I thought. This was going downhill.

Throughout the process, my voice had risen and my throat had tightened. It was feeling like an interrogation, and I was becoming more and more defensive. I resisted what I interpreted as attacks on my knowledge and identity. The truth was, of course, that nobody was attacking me. They just wanted to understand my plan, gain some information, and discuss some pitfalls. They were, in fact, actually rather kind and attentive. I, however, felt misunderstood, personally and professionally attacked, and so I reacted as if I were under assault.

By the end, I looked like a massive, angry bull in an arena, spewing steam from my big Italian nose. All the while, I was disintegrating on the inside. About twenty minutes had gone by, when Eric finally put his hands up in the shape of a T, looked at me, and said, "Roberto, should we take a short break here?" Then he smiled and said, "Would you like to take your jacket off?"

Drops of sweat were trickling down my forehead. I smiled nervously and thanked him for asking. When I took my jacket off, my light blue shirt showed stains on my chest, down the insides of my sleeves, and down my back.

When the meeting resumed, I noticed that the panel were biting their lips and holding forced smiles. I was even more embarrassed than they, and they knew it. That cocky, hot-headed Italian was facing circumstances for which he was not prepared.

The meeting ended, and in spite of my shaky performance, I got a green light on the project. As people were leaving the conference room, I gathered my documents. I unbuttoned my shirt and grabbed some paper towels to wipe my forehead. Eric smiled and thanked me. "Can't wait to see how this is going to turn out," he said. "I can tell you know your tech stuff."

Yes, I knew my tech stuff. I knew what type of interfaces I would develop, the reporting system I could create for them, down to the lines of code I needed to write. But what I didn't know, I realized at that moment, was the *people* stuff. That was an entirely different, and more confounding, interface to understand.

That meeting was one of the first and most profound times the world slapped me and told me, right to my face, right to my loud jacket and ruined shirt, that regardless of my technical prowess and methodical mind, my insolent, cocky self would not be enough to help me in the corporate world and my career.

That moment was the beginning of my journey into realizing that I had been hiding in plain sight most of my life. However good I was at resolving issues behind my monitor and on paper, using a well-organized approach, looking at problems, and offering solutions, I had been hiding in safety and avoiding experiences that could bring emotional tension and discomfort.

I knew how to consider alternatives or possible tangents and digressions, and I had trained my mind to take different perspectives into account. I was a master at analyzing, eliminating, or including possibilities. Such things were simple for me.

What I could not control and didn't understand was the deep, complicated well inside me, the mental and emotional subtext and intricacies of what makes me human. I had technical skills to the hilt, I had an enormous amount of knowledge, but I lacked emotional intelligence.

Scientists have discovered that our level of emotional intelligence is 10 percent linked to genetics, leaving the other 90 percent up to us (i.e., 10 percent nature, 90 percent nurture). The ability to deal with emotional matters is primarily influenced by the way we were raised, the culture we were born into, and the family, people, signs, songs, and symbols that surrounded us. But that's not all. "Nurture" also consists of the conscious desire and effort we put into recognizing what is happening to us and what we want to do about it.

For most of my life, I focused on external, superficial matters: how I appeared to others and how others appeared to me. But I didn't really take the time to understand, much less compassionately consider, what was going on *within* me and why things and situations would trigger me.

If something were comfortable or fun, I would go for it. Ready, fire, aim, I thought. I embraced fun and validation without much consideration for how my thoughts and actions affected others. I expected and I demanded, with zero culpability.

So, given my natural proclivities and general narcissism, if someone would do something that affected or bothered me, I would get annoyed, push back, and let them hear about it in no uncertain terms. It was easy for me to blame others when I couldn't face my own mistakes, to get offended if they reprimanded me, and to tell people off when the conversation wasn't aligned with my point of view.

But do you see the common denominator? It was all about *me*. I was defensive and unreasonable, as that was the only way I knew how to protect myself and my unhealthy, unexamined ego. We've all been through similar experiences and revelations; such is our growth as human beings. But to be a "human *being*" is to be a verb, a process of becoming human. And that, let me tell you, is one tough nut to crack. I had no idea how tough.

My general stubbornness stemmed from my avoidance to deal with my inner "stuff." Managing and understanding my emotions was hard, so, of course, I tended to take the easy route. I either bottled them up or expressed them in detrimental ways.

Overall, I did what many of us do. I lacked courage and didn't bother to look in the mirror to recognize my shit and work on it.

I didn't know it then, but I am aware of it now. Back then, I was just a cocky coward, and my cocky cowardice was like my checkered Italian jacket—it stood out and didn't look good on me. Except I didn't know it.

Even though I got the contract, that meeting proved fateful. It was a personal disaster in that my emotions were visibly triggered and I had no skillful means to deal with them. The tension I felt was a tug-of-war between my personal drive to deliver an excellent presentation (cockiness), and the cocoon of safety I created around myself to avoid any hint of emotional distress (cowardice).

I knew how to get myself out of complex predicaments on-screen, with logical lines of code and well-planned diagrams. However, when dealing with something as unpredictable as humans, with their emotions and their convoluted, multilayered, multifaceted aspects of communication, behaviors, and personalities, well, I was stumped. Boy, I had a lot to learn, starting with mining and questioning my own deep-seated issues. Over time I realized that the same problems kept appearing in different areas of my life, until I could no longer avoid seeing the truth. Get your shit together, I finally told myself, and be honest about it, even if you don't know how to fix it.

When we want to move up in the world, we want the approval of the people around us and particularly of those above us. This is a perfectly normal aspiration, as we tend to look at peers, but especially our elders and superiors, as the guides to our future and templates for success.

But when we look to others for approval, we also naturally subject ourselves to their disapproval. The fear that we will lose the support or favor of our superiors, peers, or stakeholders can be overwhelming and often debilitating.

I knew that my personal transformation would require the courage to face what triggered me and that it would have to grow from that discomfort. Laying low to avoid discomfort was simply no longer an option. How long and how many times did I want to experience awkward moments like this? And how many more shirts was I willing to ruin, literally and figuratively?

The tension I experienced often occurred in social

interactions where I primarily wanted to be safe, instead of being sincere and present. I would wonder how much I should share, for fear of being deemed uninspiring or unworthy. Were they going to judge me and my work? What would they think of me if I spoke up and contradicted others? These moments were challenging and uncomfortable. The tension made me hot and sweaty, triggering reactions, emotions, and behaviors, most of which you've doubtless experienced and/or observed in others, such as:

- smiling nervously
- being vague
- changing the subject
- avoiding eye contact
- mumbling
- having a rattle in your throat
- constantly apologizing
- racing heartbeat
- shutting down
- not listening
- feeling irritable
- procrastinating
- being passive-aggressive
- judging others
- judging yourself
- being secretive
- feeling defensive
- being aggressive
- thinking negatively
- being preoccupied
- joking/being sarcastic

All of these reactions provide emotional protection. They make you wonder if the effort of the social engagement is even worth the discomfort. So you tend to stick to the things you are familiar with, where you feel fully capable and in control on your home turf, whatever it may be. You are, in a word, hooked on your identity, and you keep falling back on it as something that feels safe, at least for the short term.

However, such protective maneuvers prevent us from expressing how we truly feel and keep our authentic self hidden. They paralyze us, making us feel intimidated, withdrawn, and cornered (just like I was in that conference room)—incapable of reaching our full potential. When we feel the need to protect ourselves, it's impossible to fully engage in life.

These days, technology makes it even easier for us to avoid dealing with our emotions and those of others. I've coached many engineers and managers, and I particularly remember one who told me that people were not happy with how he was responding to his peers. They said he was brusque and lacked communication skills. They had complained to HR and asked that HR address his offensive style before it affected the whole team.

I asked him how he expressed himself.

"Oh, I can tell you exactly what they're talking about," he said. Then, to my alarm, he took out his phone. "Let me show you the chat exchange we had."

I interrupted him and asked if he could tell me about his live-voice interactions, meaning his actual, embodied interactions—his real, human contact.

"When was the last face-to-face conversation you had with X, and how did it go?" I asked.

He looked at me dumbfounded. "I barely have any live conversations," he said. "Ninety percent of my communication is through our messaging platform."

From the tone of his voice I could tell that he didn't see any connection between his issues and his lack of live communication.

This is actually the norm today, and it's a widespread sickness. You can send messages deprived of any social and emotional touch through chat platforms or emails, and while it's efficient, all such communication reinforces the "coward" stance of staying in your cocoon and not taking any risks. Often, if a recipient misunderstands something, it's blamed on the brevity and the technology limitations—a convenient excuse for what in reality is just poor communication.

The problem is, of course, not the medium itself; the problem is that the technology allows people to remain hidden behind a mask (which is a portable wall). In the safety of our comfort zone, we can feel great about how clever, efficient, and superior we are. All the while, we remain blind to the discontent that is growing every day.

To get out of our cocoon, we must take risks, look in the mirror, and see our crap for what it is. We can't code our way to a successful career and life. Our technical skills will only get us there halfway. Your algorithms may get you through the door, but, once in, how you advance has more to do with your attitude than your business acumen.

If, however, you have the courage to work on yourself and your behavior, you will notice that not only you as a person will change but everything around you will change. I've learned from my own experience that we can leverage our current problem-solving skills and use them as a template for working with others.

When you are coding, for example, you are most likely completely focused. You can use that same single-minded focus to become present and centered when interacting with others. You probably have a good amount of confidence because you have proven that you can overcome mind-boggling challenges others would be intimidated by. You have a talent for visualization, you know how to make a process more efficient, resolve issues, and distill even the most abstract and convoluted systems into something that makes sense. These are all skills you can use in optimizing your own "system"—in transforming yourself into an inspiring leader.

For over fifteen years I worked in software development, dealing with small-to-large databases in financial corporations, managing projects from conception to close, developing applications, coding, and speaking tech. I've spent countless hours behind a screen looking for bugs, creating diagrams, and interacting with and training users and stakeholders. Only later did I come to understand that what I really needed to excel in my work was a deeper understanding of the people side of the business, and I became interested in human behavior just as much as the technical aspects. That's when I started to realize the parallels between how I used logic and coding in my programs and how I understood end users' needs. In years of working with other "technical minds," I've noticed that most of them, like me, are inspired by:

- the desire to help people
- the drive to solve problems
- using the entrepreneurial mindset to find solutions for an issue
- the persistence in finding bugs
- the enthusiasm and passion in constantly improving from the current state
- using creativity to find innovative solutions
- strategic planning
- following the logical flow of thoughts to understand facts or come to conclusions
- the focus and presence experienced in the flow
- the research and critical thinking based on facts and data

When I was a teenager in Switzerland, I'd go to the auto mechanic shops after hours, rummaging through their trash and containers of used-car parts. I enjoyed dismantling auto parts to see how they functioned. As a child, I had done the same thing with my toys. Sure, I sucked at putting them back together, but I loved the challenge. Within me, and likely within you too, there was always that innate, inherent desire to understand how things worked. The process of discovering, troubleshooting, and acquiring knowledge kept me engaged. I wanted to figure things out and create something new.

Today, that drive within me is just as alive as it was back then. The difference is that I've shifted to social interactions, people, and conversations. People are fascinating to me, and I study the tone of voice, body language, communication—all the different parts that make interactions and their outcomes so complex and compelling.

If we take the time to observe ourselves, acknowledge what is happening, and understand how our actions and our environment are closely interlinked, we can use that knowledge to transform ourselves and the way we live.

Many books talk about emotional intelligence. They all share the five core elements that Daniel Goleman presented in his 1995 book *Emotional Intelligence: Why It Can Matter More Than IQ*:

1. **Knowing one's emotions.** This is about looking inside, being OK with what you see, and understanding it.

2. **Appropriately managing these emotions.** When you know what is happening, you can control what to do with it.

3. **Motivating yourself and using your emotions to reach a goal.** Here you get to choose how you will apply this to your benefit.

4. **Recognizing emotions in others.** Through empathy, you understand others better and adapt accordingly.

5. **Handling relationships.** Now you have the skills to manage emotions about others in social contexts.

A few questions to ask yourself:

- What got you to pick up this book?
- What is your own cocoon like?
- What are some of your trigger points?

Chapter 2

What Does It Mean to "Dance"?

The dancer's instruction manual

"Life is simple. Everything happens for you, not to you. Everything happens at exactly the right moment, neither too soon nor too late. You don't have to like it . . . it's just easier if you do." —*Byron Katie*

In the early 1990s, after I moved to the Bay Area from Europe, I developed an acute interest in anything related to self-improvement—from books that covered the healing energies of the woo-woo universe to the physical and emotional practices that promised to help us become "better people." I joked that if someone walked into my apartment and saw all those self-help books on the shelves, they might wonder just how much help I needed. When I walked around a bookstore's self-help aisle, I often felt uneasy, and at the register I was afraid the cashier would judge me. Even when reading one of those books in a coffee shop, I would always make sure to hide the cover as much as possible (I'd always remove the dust jacket, if the book was hardback).

"He's reading a self-help book," I imagined others thinking. "What do you think is wrong with him?"

Well, that was one way to look at it; I was certainly in need of improvement. Another reason for the pull of these books was that I was aware that there was more to us than our mundane daily experiences. That there must be something deeper to understand about this world and, more importantly, about ourselves.

Whatever it was, I knew that I would not find it in programming and technology-related books. I had to turn to deeper sources. So I explored subjects related to causes and symptoms of illnesses or behavior, increasing intuition, energetic healing, chakras, meditation, the law of attraction—anything spiritual, really. At some point, I even owned a pendulum, although I think I trashed it about a month later—after all, I didn't want to end up living in a yurt, gazing at crystals. I wanted to apply my knowledge in practical ways.

Most of the authors I read had wise, informed perspectives on approaching life and understanding human behavior, especially when facing difficult situations. I was hungry for their knowledge and ideas; what they had to offer resonated with me deeply. But—and yes, there is a "but"—I soon realized that it was easy to talk about this stuff; applying it, however, was a whole different beast. That part was, in fact, downright frustrating and demoralizing.

Were these people sitting in a cave and meditating all day long? It's a lot easier to be a saint on a mountain than to be, as Bruce Springsteen wrote, "a saint in the city."

I'm *not* in a cave or a monastery or atop a mountain, I wanted to scream at these authors. I'm in the city—working, paying taxes, having to catch buses and deal with relationships. I am making my way through life and a career, with all the challenges that people like me face every day. On a nearly daily basis, I was facing troubles and dilemmas that couldn't be resolved with a nice quote from *The Way Within* or *The Book of Zen*.

I mostly read these books in my closet. I didn't have a coach or the right people who could help me with all of this, and not everyone was open to my out-there, self-help perspective, especially in the tech world. Like so many others, I was not comfortable sharing what was going on with me, and I believed I was strong enough to handle this transformation on my own anyway.

So I kept doing what I was doing, and life kept showing me that, well, it wasn't working. Time and time again, I found myself in situations in which I felt awkward and out of place—trapped in that metaphorical conference room, my hands sweating, with no exit.

In spite of all the amazing insights I gained from reading, my behaviors were stubbornly refusing to change; they were simply too entrenched. A nagging suspicion arose in me. What if all my soul-searching and seeking, though earnest, were ultimately just another hideout? What if it were a place that allowed me to feel accomplished and insightful without truly challenging me? I wasn't too far from living alone in a yurt, after all. And dammit, I was becoming comfortable with the idea.

I continued to read wisdom-filled books and pile up more insights, but I realized that ultimately I needed to stop hiding, gather my courage, and begin the work of self-inquiry and authentic interactions with others. I was a long way from dancing, and I knew that as long as I stayed in my chosen book-closet, I would never learn or practice it.

Have you ever felt that something was "off"?

Particularly in moments when I became defensive, or when my responses no longer matched the context, I knew that I was off, that something wasn't right.

An inappropriate response to stress is something that many of us experience, and it is never comfortable. You can physically sense the tight feeling in your chest or the tensing of your shoulders. The triggers may be hard to locate, but their power over you is not.

We all despise feeling powerless, forced to struggle, freeze, or run away. All of these reactions can cause a great deal of stress, and because this kind of stress is so hard to manage, we tend to take the easy way out and we become frustrated, angry, cowardly, or boorish. Needless to say, these are not qualities that make for a happy, healthy outlook on life. Such behaviors, in fact, only lead to regret. We think of "stressful situation X" with shame and regret ("Dammit,

I could've handled that better"), but we rarely ask *how* we could have handled the situation better. If we seriously ask that question and don't just brush it off with a commonplace phrase ("I should have stayed calm and collected"), if we really think through such questions, it can feel very threatening. It makes us realize that we are human, and as humans we are faulty. It reminds us that we don't know how to dance yet, that we still have a lot to learn.

If any of the above rings true to you, then you are reading the right book.

Everything you experience involves choices. You can decide to learn how to respond to life events in helpful, life-altering ways, and the way you respond will depend on the compounded layers of experiences, background, and culture that make you who you are. These layers are like colored glass filters that make us perceive and face the world in our unique ways. So, even before you approach the dance floor of life, your subconscious filters make you hear the low beat and vibrations of a drum, the lyrics riding on melody in ways unique to you.

These layers may help you appreciate and dance to the music, or they may distort the melody and trigger you adversely. Regardless of how they shape your perception, however, you don't have to be a passive, helpless onlooker. On the contrary, you can consciously influence and shape these layers.

Metaphorically speaking, it all begins with understanding how your filters impact the way you hear the music. Nobody can do this for you because you alone know how you connect to the music and what your experience is like.

This particular inside knowledge is unique to you, and you can explore and learn from it.

You already know what technical skills and achievements you will put on your résumé; that's the part everybody can see and check. But only you are in the position to really understand who you are deep down, and gaining that knowledge will give you all the tools you need to navigate your social interactions. It's what differentiates an expert from a leader. It's what gives you the ability to dance.

To start with, you will need to identify the defaults and patterns from which the fabric of your personality is woven. From there, you will build a map to help you charter your new path and navigate through difficult terrain. This will require courage, candor, and a lot of emotional and psychological archaeology.

The truly confident person never flaunts confidence. He or she won't roar like an ape beating its chest to establish dominance. Instead, this person will exude a casual, compassionate assuredness and will graciously inspire others through a developed, aware, and honest sense of self.

Such a person will not hide behind achievements. He or she is fully aware of being vulnerable, can ask for help, and leads others with authenticity. A mature and developed person can manage his emotions and is comfortable apologizing when having made mistakes. Enlightened leaders have a spine but never bully people. They have heart but are not driven by their emotions. They are assertive *and* have empathy.

Such people get on the dance floor in the middle of the crowd. They don't even need courage to do so, because they have no problem being seen and are able to shrug off a terrible moonwalk or awful rhythm. They can laugh at themselves when wearing either funny dance shoes or the loudest checkered Italian jacket on the planet.

The question is, how do they do this?

The answer is simple: they observe the emotions running through them, they recognize and identify them, and then they act accordingly. For those of us who haven't done the work of self-discovery yet, the sequence of events is often reversed: you feel an emotion or an impulse, you act on it, and then later, after the fact, you ask yourself what was going on. But by then, of course, you can only deal with the fallout from your action because you have missed your opportunity to freely choose the appropriate response.

None of this is magic, not by a long shot. But it *is* magical to learn a completely new way of being in this world, and to do so requires time, patience, and some pain. But, I can promise you, doing so changes everything. You will not only see the world through a whole new lens, you will see the world the way you should have all along.

Learning how to dance is not unlike learning to drive. Initially, you have to remember damn near every conscious act you make, and that can feel overwhelming and impossibly hard to maintain; only with time will your conscious actions become unconscious habits. Then you have to worry about the other drivers (read: society), not only operating all the controls and functions but doing so without getting killed or killing someone else. And yet, after a few months, driving becomes second nature.

Likewise, when you learn to dance, you need to relax into the music and be with it, without filtering its parts or analyzing every note. You won't need to force or control your movements; instead, they will flow organically from the music (read: your environment). This kind of gracefulness stems from knowing how your filters can affect you and your ability to connect with others without losing your independence or yourself.

As your own moves become more effortless, you begin to also understand the individual nuances of how others dance, and you can adapt and modify your moves accordingly. You have to pay attention to the music not just with your ears but with all your senses, experiencing its vibrations and how they affect your partners. Then and only then can you shift from solo to partner dancing, making the other feel safe, supported, and appreciated. You allow them to use their self-expression, and you jump in to guide when needed or to just dance along. In short, you are now collaborating with others in a mutual trajectory toward success.

Right now, this very second, is your time and opportunity to write your future, to learn a new, unique-to-you dance that is expressive, whole, and self-sustaining.

Cultivating your emotional intelligence and knowing how to dance will help you become exceptional at work and likewise, will help you live a fuller and more authentic life. I had to learn these steps the hard, conscious, and mindful way, and I'm more than happy to share what I've learned with you.

But before we truly start this journey, let's make sure that you are ready and willing to move forward. Do you acknowledge that our brains and talents are no more than a starting point? That, to do the real work, you need to have the belief, the dedication, and the sincere willingness to explore what you have and haven't done?

Every moment counts.

According to Daniel Goleman in his book *Social Intelligence: The New Science of Human Relationships,*[1] the top six competencies that distinguish star performers from average performers in the tech sector are, in this order:

- Strong achievement drive and high achievement standards
- Ability to influence
- Conceptual thinking
- Analytical ability
- Initiative in taking on challenges
- Self-confidence

Question:
Out of the six, only two (conceptual thinking and analytical ability) are purely intellectual competencies. The other four, including the top two, are emotional competencies.

- Which one(s) of those four do you already have?
- Which one(s) don't you have and are thus holding you back?
- Do you sometimes sense that something is off?
  And if so, are you ready for the red pill? (Or is it the blue one?)

---

[1] Daniel Goleman, *Social Intelligence: The New Science of Human Relationships* (Bantam, 2006), 43.

Chapter 3

Will You Enter the Bar?

Getting into the right mindset to dance

Imagine yourself arriving at a bar where you are supposed to meet a friend. You peek through the window to see if she is already there. The place doesn't look particularly inviting: dim lights, large flat-screen TVs, a handful of people (most of them staring at their cell phones), and no music. What a gloomy scene!

Your friend arrives, and questions arise. Should you go in, or find another place? Is the somberness of the place going to drag down your night, or will you feel cheerful regardless? Do you want to meet new people or be left alone? There are many things to ponder in just a few seconds. And then there is, of course, the final question: what will you do? Seriously, what is your gut feeling telling you? Are you going to walk away and look for a better place, or are you willing to give this bar a try?

This little scene may seem trivial, but the questions it brings up go to the heart of how we respond to life events and the decisions we make. How we answer may reveal significant truths about us.

Common wisdom has it that we can't control our environment; all we can do is control our attitude toward it. However, in my experience, this saying runs counter to a simple but important fact: when we change our perspective, we actually *do* change our environment. Sure, we can walk away from the bar, hoping there'll be something better around the corner. But what if instead we walked in, turned on some music, and struck up conversations with people? What if our energy were strong enough to light up the room, regardless of the gloom?

Several years ago, a friend and I both went through a divorce at the same time. We both made a conscious decision not to let the difficulty of it drag us down. Instead, we saw our newfound singlehood as a chance to rekindle our enthusiasm for life, and so, we went out, determined to have a good time.

And no matter where we ended up, we would turn the place around and make it a fun night. Now, I don't want to sound like some Pollyanna pretending to always be cheerful. I do not believe the world is always bright and jolly, full of butterflies and rainbows, if only we have the right mindset—not at all. I've had my share of awful moods and pessimistic outlooks, and I would never discount the suffering that we all experience in life; sometimes, the most appropriate response is to just acknowledge the pain without judging it and to be gentle and empathetic with yourself.

However, I have made many bad decisions because I showed up with the wrong attitude, and I've learned that if I pay attention to my mindset and remind myself of what I can bring to a given situation, I will affect my surroundings—regardless of how gloomy they may be.

Sure, not every change is necessarily a complete turnaround; maybe I can improve a situation by only 10 percent, but 10 percent is still a win on any metric. Particularly when it comes to working on ourselves, every percent counts.

Your attitude can quite literally change the room.

Earlier I touched on emotional intelligence. Psychologist Carol Dweck has spent her career researching why emotional intelligence (EQ) is a better predictor of success than IQ. She explains that people generally fall into one of two categories: those with a fixed mindset and those with a growth mindset.

With a fixed mindset, people believe that their basic abilities, intelligence, and talents are fixed traits. They believe that what they were born with (their intelligence, physical abilities, etc.) is basically all there is and that they will have to operate within their given limitations. They generally feel that "this is the way I am" and are unwilling or unable to conceive of themselves as having a much greater potential.

People with a growth mindset, by contrast, see skills, abilities, and attitudes as things that can change through effort, good teaching, coaching, and persistence.

Recent research on the brain's neuroplasticity has shed some interesting light on this discussion. It has revealed that we can literally rewire our brains, even as adults, by developing new habits. We can increase our EQ, for example, by paying attention to our old habits and then successively adapting new ones. We start this process by diagnosing and understanding what is keeping us in our current state and then thinking about what it would take to create new habits. The more frequently we engage in this kind of exploration, the more organic and effortless it will become. Over time, we will notice how it begins to affect our overall stance, in addition to our mental and physical state. Even the smallest actions, research shows, can increase productivity and happiness.

If you have a fixed mindset, I want to encourage you to consider the possibility that your potential is much greater than what you have allowed yourself to believe. For me, understanding how I show up in life has been a deeply personal goal. For many years, I have tried to understand my own moods and attitudes, what triggers me and what I can do to become less reactive. I've worked on enhancing my positive sides and fixing the negative ones. And yes, the understanding that needs to precede growth takes effort and self-awareness—and the patience, tolerance, and support of many people around me. And it's true that shifting your mindset is challenging because it requires you to leave your comfort zone. As Billy Anderson, author of *Your Comfort Zone Is Killing You*, writes, "Courage is being scared and doing it anyway, because the something that you want is bigger than the fear itself."

The more we confront what scares us, the less it will continue to scare us, and the less our fears will have the power to control us. Regardless of which side of the mindset you lead toward, you will benefit from self-awareness and the support of the people around you. But when we approach this journey with a growth mindset, a can-do attitude, our intrinsic beliefs will motivate us and actually propel us forward rather than limiting and restraining us.

All right, are you open and ready to grow? As a technical expert, you may still be wondering if you have what it takes to grow your EQ. The answer is a resounding yes! In fact, I'll show you how you can leverage your existing strengths within the social and emotional domain.

Here is how we are going to do this: every time I introduce a novel way of approaching a social situation, I will try to frame it in ways similar to how we approach a technical difficulty, so that we can leverage our current tools and continue to use a logical, analytical, and problem-solving approach.

Decision-making is a mysterious, multilayered phenomenon, and it is as emotional as it is logical. Neuroscientists are in alignment on this fact and describe it clearly.[2] To decide something, you "sense" it first and then you look at rational data to support your initial gut feeling. Every decision we make is genuinely a gut feeling backed by logic, not vice versa. Even the most hard-core neuroscientist will tell you that our logical system and emotional system are inseparably linked.

(By the way, if this alone turns you off, you are probably having an emotional reaction to what I'm sharing. As a rational, thinking person, it might bug you to think that emotions drive decisions. If this is the case, please bear with me and remember that we are trying to adopt a growth mindset. Don't walk out of the bar yet, because you *can* change the room with your attitude. If not right now, then soon.)

While logic is part of a decision process, your gut feelings and what you sense in your heart will ultimately have more power. Mind and heart are not mutually exclusive, but we primarily live on instinct. Most of our waking lives, we operate below the level of conscious awareness. As a result, much of how we behave is reactive and unintentional.

As human beings, we tend to make decisions based on learned stereotypes, attitudes, and other types of categorization. Doing so makes us feel safe and gives us templates to better navigate how we interact with others.

---

[2] Alan Watkins, *Coherence: The Secret Science of Brilliant Leadership* (Kogan Page, 2013), 107.

For example, the Halo Effect is a cognitive bias in which one's overall impression of a person influences how we feel about their character. Our judgment of another's exterior, if we aren't fully mindful, informs our notions of their inner selves and agency.

Equally powerful, and inherent in our very evolution, is the Confirmation Bias, wherein we tend to favor information that fits with our own preexisting experience, ideas, and beliefs. Furthermore, as if we didn't have enough inherent biases working against us all the time, there is the Affinity Bias, which leads us to connect with others who share similar backgrounds, experiences, and interests, and causes us to dismiss others who are not like-minded. All of these biases can unconsciously affect our choices and will hence impact our work and how we engage with (or avoid) people.

Let's look at a real-life example from one of my coaching clients that shows us how we need to train and use both our logical and emotional capacities to really understand a situation.

Let's call him George. He's an engineer in Silicon Valley working on highly innovative concepts. With over twenty years of experience in his field, he is highly regarded.

George often worries about what other people might think of him and his work. For example, if he writes code and later finds bugs, he takes it so personally that he is consumed by remorse. He says things like, "I can't believe I made these errors. They must think I'm a total loser, and they probably won't give me other projects to lead."

He dwells on these worries and engages in what we say in Italian, *farsi i film in testa,* which translates as "making movies in your head." He obsessively replays worst-case scenarios. Like so many of us, George has become accustomed to imagining scenes that are based not on facts but on his fears. In his case, the fears stem from a deep-seated anxiety of not being good enough or smart enough for his peers.

In order to break the cycle of negative emotions, I tried to trigger George's logical, rational mind by asking questions like:

• What makes you think you are a loser?

• Have people told you that you are a loser?

• Why do you think you won't be given more projects to lead?

• On what are you basing your emotional response?

I wanted George to use a fact-based analysis to understand how his thought processes had been hijacked by unfounded assumptions. When in the throes of an emotional response, it is key to break it down with elements that are undeniable and factual; this is a process known as cognitive restructuring. Methodologically, this process is not unlike what George would do when developing a solution for one of his programs: break it down into its elements, precisely define the steps and procedures that have been used, and then restructure the individual elements in a way that better aligns with the objective, free of groundless assumptions.

If you had to use coding syntaxes to problem-solve, you would use a series of statements, such as:

- **If...Then...Else**, allowing conditional execution based on the expression's evaluation

- **For Each...Next**, repeating a group of statements for elements in an array or collection

- **For...Next**, repeating a group of instructions a specific number of times

- **Select Case...End Case**, conditionally executing one or several statement blocks, depending on the expression's value

This is, of course, simplified, and I could go on with many more variations, but you get the point. The approach is no different from what a programmer or scientist does when using logic to discover a process, analyze data, or write lines of code to address a problem.

It was easy for George to visualize his emotional response by creating a diagram on paper that followed the same methodology he uses in coding. We then used the same strategy to analyze the circumstances, personalities, and desired outcomes of conversations. No matter what the discovery process, this method enabled him to tackle a predicament rationally and get him out of the false and misleading screenplay in his head.

You have most likely already seen the diagram below. As simple as it is, it is incredibly difficult to put into practice. As you read this book, I invite you to draw similar "solution diagrams" to understand what is holding you back and to then find a path forward.

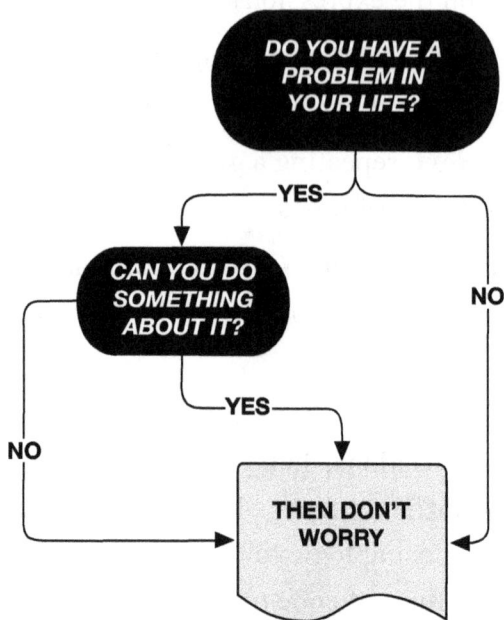

So, here you are again, standing on the curb, in front of that bar. You might still be looking inside and pondering your next move. You are asking yourself questions and reflecting on their consequences. And while you are logically exploring what to do, your emotions are competing with your reason. But because you are conscious of your emotions, you will now be able to make a more aware and honest choice.

But even with the best rational process, no matter what you choose, there are risks involved. This is, I believe, where the growth mindset will prove very helpful. If you don't want to risk anything, you risk even more. Not entering that bar will reinforce a safe, fixed mindset. Conversely, walking into the bar with confidence and openness will lead to a multitude of possibilities. Sure, some of them may not work out, but by opening up new possibilities (rather than staying in your comfort zone) you increase your chances for success and you learn a lot about yourself, your level of awareness, your propensity for risk-taking, and your desire for growth.

Chapter 4

Grow, or Live to Regret It

*Will you choose to take
the first dance step?*

A few years back, I was seeing a therapist, mostly for relationship issues, but even then I knew that my romantic troubles were part of a larger issue.

The therapist knew me well, and I enjoyed our sessions. But in one particular session, she asked me, seemingly out of nowhere, "Roberto, do you ever ask for help when you are facing difficulties?"

"Of course," I replied. "I don't mind doing that at all."

"That's great," she said. "So, tell me, how would you

ask your partner for help?"

"I don't know. I'd just ask."

"OK, good. Go ahead and say it out loud, right now. How would you ask her for help?"

I started to get a bit irritated. "What do you mean?" I said. "It's pretty straightforward, no? If I don't know how to do something, or if I'm overwhelmed, I'll just ask her."

"I understand, Roberto," my therapist said in a gentle but firm way. "I would just like you to say it out loud. Go ahead and ask her right now. Tell her that you need help."

"OK, fine," I said, feeling a bit silly. "Here goes. 'Isabel, I need your help . . .'" And the moment these words left my mouth, I choked. My eyes welled up with tears and I couldn't finish the sentence.

Good *Lord*. I had no idea what was happening. Why on earth had I become so emotional? I looked at my therapist.

"Tougher than you thought, isn't it?" she said, smiling.

The truth is that I didn't even know that I had been stuck in this way. My girlfriend and I had difficulties in our relationship, sure, but I didn't have the slightest inkling that something so basic as articulating my needs sincerely and out loud were holding me back.

When I told my therapist this, she said, "Well, you only find out when you actually try."

That line was a seismic moment for me, as profound as it was simple: *You only find out when you actually try.* Unless we go out there, take action, and risk exposing ourselves, we may never even understand how stuck we are, much less *who* we are.

Children have an innate desire to learn, grow, experiment, and experience. You probably don't have to think too far back to remember when you were pining away for the next adventure, the next challenge, something that inspired you and made you feel glad to be alive.

Now take a moment to look at your life as it is today. Chances are, if you are reading this book, there are things that are not working out as you would like them to. Maybe you are not advancing in your career and feel stuck. Perhaps you allow events to control you, rather than taking charge of events. Maybe you sense there is a more aware you inside of you but you don't know how to access it. Whatever the nature of your concern, it shows that you carry a desire for openness and growth in you, but something is holding you back, likely because your old habits consume you before you can move forward.

Most likely it is you who are responsible for where you are right now. But don't worry, you are not permanently stuck.

Change begins with our choices. Imagine your life as a chess game, filled with millions of possibilities. Every move you make creates alternative outcomes now and in the future. Your life contains just as many possibilities, and every decision will produce different results. When you make a choice, an irreversible variant occurs, which in turn leads to further variations. (So, if you look at it this way, it's courageous to even leave the house at all.)

Of course, you could decide to not make any moves and play it safe, but that would mean stalling the game, and by stalling you only deny yourself the possibility of creating new variants that could lead to positive results. But what if instead you went the opposite way? What if you nurtured your life force and its innate need for expansion? What if you acquired new knowledge and skills through education and took some risks? By education, I also mean self-discovery, where you obtain solutions within yourself and are willing to explore other possibilities for growth.

When we start something new, it often produces a mix of exhilaration and tension. I'm sure you have experienced the feeling when you've started a new job, a new relationship, or a trip to a foreign place. You can feel it coursing through you, this excitement that is almost difficult to distinguish from fear, that sense of heightened curiosity and keen attentiveness.

It is the energy of renewal. Taking these self-driven steps to improve your career, health, relationship, and yourself will release that trapped energy that was previously stagnant and unavailable. It will greatly help you to confront personal issues and roadblocks you no longer want to tolerate.

It is easy to feel regret about the lives we are not living, to miss that which might have been, to wish we had loved more, worked harder, saved more money, traveled, stayed on the soccer team, or studied harder. Our regrets can become endless and maddening if they take the form of "what if" and lead us away from the far more important question "Well, that was then, but what *now*?"

It takes no effort to wish you had married that person or walked away from that relationship, done more yoga, or smoked less. It's easy to miss the friendships we didn't take time to make, to wish we'd made that phone call, or to regret waiting so long to visit family. In short, it's easy to regret and keep regretting, day in and day out, mourning the lives that you didn't lead. But the problem is regret itself. You can never know if there could have been a better or worse version of yourself. You cannot change the past, but this doesn't mean you have to stay stuck in a loop or leading a redundant, undiscovered life. So it's time to take a good look in the mirror and notice the gap between where you are now and who you want and truly need to be.

Sure, what we see in that mirror can be intimidating and can create feelings of inadequacy and shame, but this is the "moment" when we get to choose whether we want to repress our fears or look at our fears as possibilities. As Brené Brown writes in *Gifts of Imperfection*, "Authenticity is a collection of choices that we have to make every day. It's about the choice to show up and be real. The choice to be honest. The choice to let our true selves be seen."

There should be no shame in having shortcomings. I've screwed up, big-time and often, and each time I chose to retreat, I perpetuated and reinforced my ineptitudes, and, in doing so, wasn't an easy man to work with. To change this, I needed to have compassion for myself and have no shame in sharing my vulnerability. Sharing vulnerability is a courageous act, by no means a cowardly one.

I had a hard time asking for help. Expressing my needs made me feel "found out." I fretted that showing that I was a human being with fears and needs would make me appear weak and leave me exposed. Overcoming this was hard. I needed to involve others in my growth and allow them to provoke or jar my thinking, to show me what I was doing and who I was.

Initially, it'll be hard. Your old ways and years of conditioning are going to require a lot of energy, maturity, and perseverance to overcome. It gets easier with time. Like a rocket ship, you will need most of your fuel in the first few minutes of takeoff. Getting free from gravity is where most of the energy is expended.

Yet it's so hard to "launch" because everything wants to stay in a state of rest. As Newton's First Law of Motion states, a body at rest tends to remain at rest, and a body in motion tends to stay in motion, unless acted on by an external force. You'll need a lot of energy and motivation to get in motion, along with a desire to let go of your ego, accept your mistakes, and apologize. Once you build that momentum, it can open a wide range of possibilities where you feel more comfortable discussing your journey and sharing your inner being with all its facets.

Decide to make new choices and follow a goal for yourself. Then, continue to put these choices in motion and see how doing so reinforces new behaviors. Finally, repeat these behaviors until you begin to unconsciously integrate them into who you are—that's when you'll start to dance with them.

Humans, at their essence, have a calling to serve and to lead in various ways. And while you might not consider yourself a leader because you are not the CEO of a large corporation, you apply leadership every day in many aspects of your life. Whether you are parenting, playing sports, organizing a party, or remodeling your kitchen, you are leading. You interact with others and lead them through encouragement, direction, and mentoring until you get the desired outcome. And, of course, to be trusted, understood, and able to relate, you need to be authentic.

So here we are, with a simple choice: either live in regret or choose to put your rocket ship in motion, despite the force of gravity.

Ask yourself: What are the things you typically regret? What have you done, or not done, that cause you to feel regret or embarrassment? Psychological studies[3] have shown that we more often regret the things we have *not* done because we tend to rationalize action over inaction, and the consequences of inaction are limitless.

Well, what's left to do, folks? *Take more risks.* This is your chance to set some goals and create new limits. How many times are you willing to take a risk every day, week, month, or year? How about right now? It could heal a relationship, create a new one, or change the course of your career.

I know you have started many projects in the past, and, like most of us, you've probably failed many times. But, as Oscar Wilde said, "Experience is the name we give to our mistakes." We are all experts at failing. We fall when we learn to walk, we crash when we learn to ride our bike. Come on, you know how to get up again.

I'm not asking you to drive your car recklessly or risk your life needlessly; that's the wrong type of risk. I'm

---

[3] Sonja Lyubomirsky, *The Myths of Happiness: What Should Make You Happy, but Doesn't, What Shouldn't Make You Happy, but Does* (Penguin Books, 2013), 226. (See more at the end of the chapter.)

asking you to try the uncharted road, try a different way, and see what you are able to make happen. I'm asking you to break your habits and nurture your innate desire to grow.

Sure, to initiate change, you'll have to confront your discomfort—but, as my therapist said, "You only find out when you actually try."

Questions:

- What risks are you willing to take to gain personal growth?
- With whom could you engage and create meaningful relationships?

Footnotes:

Sonja Lyubomirsky, *The Myths of Happiness: What Should Make You Happy, but Doesn't, What Shouldn't Make You Happy, but Does* (Penguin Books, 2013)

Sonja Lyubomirsky, in her book *The Myths of Happiness*, explains it in four points:

Rationalizing action is easier than rationalizing inaction. You can regret taking a job or marrying your spouse, or you can live in the regret of not having taken that opportunity for the rest of your life.

Regret over inaction magnifies over time. That person we married or that opportunity we grabbed can show up as a big failure pretty fast, but the ones we didn't pursue can be more troubling and painful over a longer period of time.

The consequences of inaction are limitless. Picking that house or buying the Porsche can expose us to the consequences of our unwise decisions very clearly. Conversely, not making any decisions makes us ruminate about all that could have happened—again, making mental movies that can hold our development back.

Blame it on the Zeigarnik effect.[4] This occurs when an activity that has been interrupted may be more readily recalled. People remember unfinished or interrupted tasks better than completed tasks. In other words, you'll be more regretful for inaction than for action (i.e., you didn't seize the moment and now can't stop thinking about it).

---

[4] https://en.wikipedia.org/wiki/Zeigarnik_effect

Chapter 5

Who Are You?

Getting to know the dancer

As an Italian, I know what it's like to enjoy *la dolce vita,* European life—to take many vacations and get ample paid time off. It's the Western European way, for the most part.

Accordingly, I was raised with the mindset that one works to live, not that one lives to work. When European businesses close for their annual four-week vacation, they are not joking, and no one bats an eye. Some companies even mandate employee holidays, knowing that a periodically rested and refreshed person will be more productive and innovative than an employee who, in the American fashion, is often ground to demoralized dust.

When I moved to the United States in 1992, I immediately noticed how people tended to work hard, for long hours, and, worst of all, considered working late nights and weekends a badge of honor, something to be praised for.

Often, people in this country view hard work as a means to getting promoted or growing in their careers. While this is understandable, it unfortunately implies being constantly connected to work. Due to peer pressure, or lack of confidence, an always-on, always-connected culture has become the norm. And it will not go away anytime soon.

Now, I've always appreciated the opportunities that this country has offered me, and I believe that working hard and smart is key to success. However, working longer hours does not necessarily lead to better output. In fact, research has shown that productivity declines sharply when people work more than fifty hours a week.

In his book *The Untethered Soul*, Michael Singer writes, "Life itself is your career, and your interaction with life is your most meaningful relationship."

Is this the case for you?

Here is a simple question I've been asking my clients: "Who are you?" By which I mean: "What constitutes your personality and the essence of who you are?"

Too heavy? Let me put it this way.

Suppose I asked you, or someone who knows you well, to give me five words or short sentences about you, your character and personality, about who you are at the core, but they couldn't mention anything related to your work. What would they say? Could they even answer such a question?

If you created more space in your life, what would

you actually fill it with? Would it be another work project? Or would it be space for writing a book, traveling, seeing friends, or enjoying some solitude?

So, the question is: What do you want more of, that makes you feel fulfilled?

After meeting with hundreds of clients, I've come to see that accomplished, so-called successful people have *become* their work and lost their identity to their career.

Have you ever been so consumed by your work that everything around you becomes just background noise? Have you ever become so lost in your task that the world shrinks into a shapeless, foggy backdrop, dull and without texture? What I mean by "identity loss" is when your life and career have meshed together with unclear boundaries, to the point where you, at your essence, have disappeared in the ether and become part of the background noise.

If I had to ask you this question again, instead of "Who are you?" I would ask, "Where are you? Can you clearly see yourself in the light, or are you lost somewhere in the fog?"

To explain this better, let me give you a couple of examples.

John, twenty-six, is a well-regarded sales account director who recently got a promotion. He was offered the opportunity to move to the East Coast to assume a new role as the director of a team of forty. He is highly qualified and has managed smaller teams before. There is no doubt that he will succeed.

But as he and I met every couple of weeks, I got to know more about him and the pressure this new position had added to his life. John was experiencing stress, sleepless nights, long workdays, and poor health habits. Occasionally, he would go to the gym or exercise. On weekends he would catch up on chores, but he dedicated Sunday evenings to planning the week ahead and answering email.

Heather, thirty-seven, is an accomplished store manager. She has worked in several high-end boutiques and has built a reputation for bringing top results. Highly qualified, she manages a team of fourteen. She meets her numbers and goes beyond, month after month, year after year.

With all of this, she has gained the reputation of being extremely well organized with high standards for herself and her team. A strong and confident leader, she is considered a person of foresight and vision, astute and ambitious. On her days off, she'll spend a few hours taking care of her home and herself, but she is always only minutes away from her email and work issues.

Both clients completed a 360 survey to solicit feedback on their performance from several different sources: their managers, their peers, and their direct reports. Here is some of the feedback John and Heather received from their teams:

Q: How often do you schedule time to think?

A: *Once a month or never.*

Q: How often do you struggle with managing your emotions when things get tough?

A: *Twice a week at least, mostly daily.*

Q: In what areas could you improve your management skills?

A: *Handling stressful situations, being more patient, being calm, monitoring my attitude and reactions, and not being so emotionally overwhelmed. Before reacting, allowing myself time to digest the situation and then formulate proper responses. Understanding how my mood can affect the rest of the team. It would help if I took the time to listen more.*

Now, let's not forget that people like John and Heather are often referred to coaching because they are high achievers whom the companies want to keep employed. They need "adjustments" because their behaviors and attitude are affecting their relationships with their peers, direct reports, customers, and the organization.

When I do coaching for a business, I am usually supplied with a list of observations that either HR or upper management have identified about my clients. They often prioritize things like developing leadership skills, improving communication, and managing a team.

What always strikes me is that the following two points are *never* addressed in such diagnostics:

- How employees tend to accept and internalize unreasonably high demands and goals imposed by their employers to the point that they neglect personal values

- How work relationships suffer when overachievers surrender their identity to their career

I see these two points in clients frequently, particularly among younger workers. And when I find evidence of either outcome, I ask them the question, "Who are you?"

Usually I'm met with silence and deer-in-the-headlights stares, followed by, "What do you mean?"

So I rephrase: "Who are you without using labels, roles, or job achievements to define yourself?"

More silence, and then they often begin listing things: "I'm a director, manager, I have sold millions, I have two degrees and seven certifications."

I interrupt: "That's not what I'm asking. Those are your awards, labels, and achievements. I would like you to tell me who you are without all that. You, John, and you, Heather."

They pause, and I can sense their struggle. They are being asked questions that larger society rarely asks.

As I wait in silence, slowly the words start coming out of them with adjectives instead of nouns: "I'm determined, passionate, funny, reluctant, self-doubting, loyal. I get triggered when people are not honest with me. I'm afraid of what others think of me. Sometimes I feel like an impostor. I need social connections. I'm an introvert. I love the feeling of belonging. I'm filled with joy when . . ."

Now we are getting somewhere.

Then I ask, "How often do you think about such things, like needing a feeling of belonging?"

Answer: "Umm, never really. Right now, I guess."

The discussion continues, with more exploration of questions like:

• What do you consider to be your role in this world?

• Who are you now? Who would you like to become?

• What is the real you without all these attachments? What if we took them all away?

- How do you feel? What do you appreciate about yourself?
- How do others make you feel about yourself?

The point is to start reflecting on who you are today and what brought you to your current position.

Think about your culture, how you grew up, your perceptions, and how all this alters how you observe the world around you. When I ask them these questions, they slowly realize that their identity is attached to their careers, achievements, successes, and failures, but little else. They feel high when they achieve a goal, and they feel low when they fail. They understand how addicted they have become to external validation and professional recognition, and they begin to see that they are dependent on extrinsic factors and lack connection to intrinsic motivators.

Extrinsic motivation causes pressure and stress, which, compounded with the lack of self-awareness and self-care, will trigger poor behavior, adverse emotional reactions, and difficulty connecting with others. This is consistent with the feedback that colleagues tend to express in the 360 survey.

Usually, after having this conversation (which does involve rigor and risk), there is a long pause. I remain quiet as the workers shift in their chair, pondering what was just said. I watch them go from a forward-leaning position to reclining. They exhale, and, once they process their answers and feelings about them, they invariably say, "Wow, I can *see* that. So, now what?"

Then I have them look at the list of behaviors they

initially decided to work on and I ask, "How many of these behaviors are triggered by what we just discussed?" They slowly begin to realize that most negative behaviors stem from their issues around extrinsic motivation. They feel that they could handle problems better if they didn't put so much pressure on themselves, weren't so lost in the fog of work, and paid more attention to their values.

Then we start identifying ways to pay more attention to our values, and actions that support those values. The employee begins by answering the questions above.

Here are some of the steps we go on to discuss:

Don't lose yourself in your career. I admire the achievements of driven people and their accomplishments. However, if such achievements come at the cost of their mental and physical health, as well as a loss of identity, are they worth it?

As you go through your work life, remember to pause and take time to exercise, spend time alone, ponder life—or just breathe. What would it take for you to move forward and out of the fog, to pay more attention to your personal life? What do you need to let go of? How comfortable are you letting things go and achieving greater balance between your work and your social and spiritual life? What could be the benefit of your finding such a balance?

I offer these questions for reflection purposes, knowing full well that they are hard to answer, much less put into practice. You need to genuinely want to find that intrinsic motivator to start shifting your priorities and put *you* in the plan, just as much as you plan for your work projects.

Reflect on what works for *you*. We all have different languages and ways to connect with our essence, the parts of ourselves that make us feel alive, enthusiastic, eager for more. What is something that made you feel that way in the past? What is the *you* project that ignites a spark and lights you up, that helps you reconnect with yourself and your values?

Learn about your character strengths. When I run a 360 survey, I often ask my client's colleagues: "If you had to tell [insert coworker's name here] about a talent, a superpower, that she has and that you wish she'd recognize in herself and use more often, what would that be?"

I then share the answer with my client and help them reflect on it. Simply seeing a talent noted by another person often allows the client to recognize it for the first time and then honor that talent.

So, feel free to ask your peers, friends, or family the same question. They probably see in you something you don't notice or refuse to examine.

Another way to get a "strengths diagnosis" is to take a Character Strengths Self-Assessment (I keep a list of on-line assessments on my website). The more time you spend discovering parts of yourself that you have disregarded, repressed, or never acknowledged, the more you'll know about areas of yourself that need your attention and that you could use to your advantage.

Let your mind flow. A mentor coach once told me: "If you put a person in front of a lamppost and ask them to talk to it for one hour, they'll come to a lot of realizations on their own."

That might sound a bit silly, I know, but it's really a thought experiment about focus and the need to let your mind wander. If you spend time alone and daydream, your daydreams can assist you in thinking things through. If you daydream while walking, that's even better, as research has shown that walking enhances creativity. So go for a long drive or a solo hike. Or, if necessary, start smaller. Maybe walk to work, or, when on the bus or train, don't look at your cell phone; look out the window and let your mind flow. You can also write in a journal; the simple act of putting pen to paper can be quite thought-provoking.

Do something with your hands and body. Get out of your mind and into your body. Garden, paint, fix something, create, build, design, you name it. As you do this, you'll get a chance to free your mind from thoughts and let your mind wander.

Observe what you sense. Notice what thoughts come to you and watch them without judgment. See how physical activity can mitigate your mental stressors. Allow realizations to present themselves to you.

Those emails and lines of code can wait. If it's your day off, make it a day off. You might want to answer those emails on Saturday morning, but, heaven forbid, what if you didn't? Or what if you waited another twelve hours before you responded? Sometimes there are urgent deadlines, but that's not what I'm talking about here. I'm referring to those tasks that can wait. And if we're honest with ourselves, we'll realize that a lot of tasks can wait.

If you find yourself pulled to the demands of your job at the expense of your quality of life, it most likely stems from your having lost your identity to your profession in such a way that it has become a threat to your habitual life. Breaking habits is a challenge for everyone, especially after practicing your technical skills for so long.

Over time, you'll get more comfortable with breaking habits and realizing what things can wait, for the sake of your own well-being.

And besides, none of your colleagues probably appreciate getting emails on a Saturday. In fact, they probably loathe them and respond only out of obligation and habit.

Nourish your mind and get inspired by traveling and reading. If you want to better understand what you are going through and how you fell into specific behaviors, expose yourself to new places and different cultures. The new environment will let you more easily recognize habitual behaviors and give you perspective on how things could be done differently.

Reading is another way to change the "environment" of your mind. At the end of this book you will find my top recommendations for additional reading to gain more insight into yourself.

Then, if you can, get some real time off, not just a long weekend or a week's vacation, but a long break. There is something magical and transformative about long breaks;

they reset your mind, refresh your thinking, and generate innovative ideas.

I've taken these extended breaks many times, and I've noticed that it takes me about two weeks to detach from the old routine and simply "be." In the third week, when you have created some distance from your old patterns and allowed insights to come through, then the magic begins to happen. That's when you start interacting with real life.

Give it a try! You have very little to lose—except your old, comfortable habits.

Ultimately, however, it is up to you and you alone to create a new you by understanding what is holding you back, by developing emotional intelligence, and by realizing your full potential. You can read this book, get coaching, and have all kinds of amazing realizations but not do anything about it. If you don't take care of yourself, your old world will keep knocking again and again.

We alone are responsible for our decisions and choices. Maybe you have never "chosen" to end up in this position, maybe you just forgot or neglected to tend to your essence and values.

Maybe the true you has slowly and over time faded into the background, obscured by the fog of anxiety and societal expectation. While it's easy to blame the universe, I believe that if you spend time honestly reevaluating your priorities, you'll realize that ultimately the choice is up to you.

So why on earth do so many of us work so hard at turning ourselves into business professionals (and perfectionists) first, and human beings second (if at all)?

You have the skills to succeed at business, this much is clear. So why not apply those same skills to your personal and emotional life? You *can*, and you know this. You just have to prioritize your own identity and essence over others' perceptions and projections. If you don't, you might look back someday and ask yourself, was it all worth it?

And then you'll be confused and wondering what the hell *it* was in the first place.

There are a lot of things that are out of your control. In fact, most things are beyond your control other than how you respond to them—the weather, the traffic, others' behavior. But again, what *is* in your control is how you choose to perceive things, how you choose to live your life, and what you will do about your future. People will only respect you more if you have the guts to be 100 percent yourself and honor the essential values important to you.

You are not defined by your work. After all, only *you* define who *you* are. You just have to start believing this is true.

Chapter 6

Kintsugi Yourself

*Learning how to dance
can be messy*

The Japanese art of kintsugi is a method of repairing broken pottery by mending the areas of breakage with gold or other metals. In this way, the breakage and repair become part of the history and evolution of the object; an object's scars are actually celebrated in this art. Kintsugi is about embracing the flaws and imperfections as a value rather than a blemish.

If you could apply this technique to your life's journey, how might this change the way you perceive yourself and others?

A few years ago, Leila, a data scientist in her mid-thirties working for a prominent Silicon Valley corporation, was asked by her company to work with a coach. Her core challenges were relationship issues with colleagues and upper management. Leila was managing a team of fifteen direct reports. She was ambitious and very knowledgeable, an expert in her field. As a female director, she had established her credibility among her male peers but still felt she had to be incommensurately assertive in order to maintain her status.

Over time, Leila's need for appreciation for her company contributions started to manifest as resentment toward her peers. This resentment would show up in her communication style and attitude. If someone said something about her work, she would feel criticized and become defensive. If her team didn't share something with her, she would wonder if they were deliberately holding back, which caused her to feel judged and anxious about herself and work.

As time went by, her resentments hardened into judgments and biases toward her peers, which affected the way she interacted with them. It even became difficult for her to attend regular meetings and share her ideas. Her colleagues sensed the tension, felt awkward, and were reluctant to approach her in conversation for fear of igniting an argument.

In our sessions, it became clear that her perceptions of her coworkers—particularly how she thought they viewed her—were clearly a distortion of the truth and one of the reasons for her distrust. Something had to change.

Misconception of others is a phenomenon that I've seen frequently in my work, and that I, too, have been guilty of. I don't think I've ever known anyone who hasn't harbored some misconceptions about another person (or about themselves).

We all have triggers that can make us fall into the trap of overthinking and misunderstanding our reality. Whenever we fall into patterns that can cause anxiety or affect what is happening, we need to be rational and get our facts straight. This is the moment when we have to use our logical and factual mindset to help overcome a "processing error."

Moreover, I've often had clients admit that their direct communication style stemmed from their biases about another's knowledge and credibility. If they don't perceive the other person as capable, it will manifest in a curt tone and a dismissive attitude toward them.

Leila had observed this behavior in herself. When I asked her how she thought she could change these biases, she said that while she could try to work on changing her perceptions of her coworkers and address them differently, she was not sure she even wanted to do that.

Initially, that was a surprise to me. But when I pried more into it, she explained that changing the way she saw them and realizing that the other person was, in reality, a reasonable person would mean that she had held the wrong perceptions all along. That, to her, would be even harder to face—the fact that she had chronically misjudged her coworkers.

I thought that was a hugely telling statement. First of all, I was grateful for and appreciative of her honesty and authenticity; that is the first step to transformation. Secondly, it taught me that while we needed to talk about her biases, we had to start by discussing her self-judgment.

All external judgment begins with internal judgment. We judge others in the same way we judge ourselves, often harshly and unforgivingly. If I believe that someone is not competent, or is a bad communicator, I usually hold some version of the same judgment toward myself.

I've learned over time that self-judgment is often done unconsciously, and because looking at ourselves might reveal aspects of our personalities that we are not ready to address yet, it's easier for us to point fingers at someone else. Research explains this mindset clearly: when people experience a setback at work, or don't finish a project on time, or face a customer complaint, they either become defensive or blame someone else for their shortcoming.

To heal from judging others and ourselves, we need to look at and focus on our own shadows and learn to accept ourselves with compassion. If we want to stop casting stones outwardly, we have to stop casting stones inwardly.

Most people I talk to are like myself, driven by an innate desire to resolve problems and help others. And yet, we don't practice enough self-care and compassion. Self-compassion means treating ourselves with the same energy, kindness, and care we would for someone we love. If you're exhausted, overworked, or stressed out, and the first thing you do when you come home after work is have a drink or crash on the sofa, you may help yourself unwind and temporarily ease the pressure, but you are not ultimately nourishing yourself, you are not resetting your mind and getting new inspiration. There is nothing wrong with relaxing over a drink, but doing so is not really giving yourself much love at all.

Why wouldn't you be more compassionate with your-self? Why wouldn't you want to treat yourself better? No wonder it is difficult for you to be empathetic with others if you treat yourself that way. Only if you feel compassion for yourself, compassion for and understanding of others can follow.

Paul Gilbert, the founder of the Compassionate Mind Foundation, maintains that compassion, while difficult and powerful, is also infectious and potentially world-changing. From my experience and my own transition into being more self-compassionate, I can tell you that kindness toward oneself *works*. And once you have started to look within yourself and have become more understanding and com-passionate toward your own shortcomings, it's essentially impossible not to see others through that same lens.

So, how does self-compassion work?

It's actually pretty simple. In the early stages, I would usually have to go through a mental process of judgment— "Oh crap, I messed up!"—followed by a series of Italian swear words, of course. But then I learned to pause, take a breath, and make a conscious effort to let go of the frustra-tion and self-resentment. Now, my old habits were so deeply engrained that this wasn't always easy (and I still some-times fail at it); high emotion and anger can be overwhelm-ing. But over time it gets easier and easier, and eventually it becomes second nature.

I remind myself to move into compassion just as I would

remind someone else. I say things like, "It's OK, buddy, don't worry. Shit happens." This compassionate self-talk has helped me develop a sense of warmth and ease, a recognition of my failures as a normal and inevitable part of life. As a result, I'm able to respond with greater clarity and more compassion toward others and see their imperfections differently.

Now let's move on to the practice.

Keep in mind that the way we think about situations or people tends to affect how we approach them. For example, if we dislike working with Mary, the project manager, we might anticipate an unpleasant conversation whenever she comes around. If we dread a conference call with our manager, chances are our mind will find all their faults and shortcomings during the meeting.

Preconceived ideas can be destructive to relationships, generate conflict, and create negative experiences for us, particularly when little to none of what we believe about others is factual. Even if you have data indicating that person X is in fact unreliable, it doesn't mean your preconceptions cannot change. You are the only person who can control yourself, your perceptions, and your biases; it is up to you to change how you show up around person X.

There is a way to "prevent" your reactions by changing your mindset. Please take the time to reflect on the following points:

- Think of a person who pushes your buttons.
- Now take a minute to dwell on that person and think about all the negative things that come to mind.

- Grab a piece of paper and draw two columns.
- In column one, write every negative thought that comes to mind.

OK, guess what? Now I'm going to ask you to change your viewpoint about that person.

Don't roll your eyes yet. Just remember that most people are not all good or all bad. To help you proceed with this, here is something that I've discovered with every client I've ever worked with—every single one, without exception. Over time, as we establish trust, they all become more transparent and vulnerable. And behind all the protective barriers they've erected around themselves, I invariably discover a human being with a beautiful heart who is kind, has good intentions, and wants to belong.

Here's an example: Imagine you are driving home during rush hour in heavy traffic. Suddenly, you see a vehicle cutting you off, someone driving like a maniac, shifting from one lane to another. What an asshole, you might think. How inconsiderate.

However, what if you then found out that driver was en route to the hospital, because his or her child was in the emergency room? That would shift your view completely, wouldn't it? You would probably move over and create space for the car, if you knew all the facts.

Or imagine that the driver who cut you off is having the worst day of his or her life. Imagine being in a similar situation and emotional state. Such empathetic imagining can truly change your mindset. Consequently, your emotions can change from anger to empathy to caring and being of assistance. You have reframed your thinking within a few seconds of cultivating empathy and imagination.

Now let's return to that person who annoys you and your list of their negative traits. Think about the person again, and now try to think of any positive traits they might have. See what comes up and take a couple of minutes to write a few words or phrases in column two. When I am doing this exercise with clients or in a classroom, participants sometimes struggle to find positive things to write, but by simply reframing their thoughts, most people can come up with at least two or three positive characteristics.

Now, the next time you interact with that person, remember what you wrote in column two. Also, notice any tension that you release. How does thinking of the positive words impact your perceptions of the person? How different could it be if you focused your attention on column two (the positive traits) rather than column one (the negative traits) when you interacted with the person?

This exercise might seem trivial, but trust me, it works. It's an example of cognitive restructuring. The change is incremental. Initially, you'll feel less tension in your body, and you'll show up calmer and more willing to interact. The other person might sense your ease and start acting differently around you.

The result is that you won't be triggered as often, and you will be more likely to end a meeting with the person on a positive note. It will get better and better each time. And gently, with practice, you'll see a change in your energy and in theirs. It is not always easy, but it's well worth a try.

Remember Leila? She was also reluctant to do this. Still, as she worked through this practice of adding self-compassion and changing her perceptions of others, people noticed a change in her attitude and behavior, and they were more inclined to work with her and praise her work.

Leila didn't need to shrink away, be less assertive, or change herself drastically. She only had to change some of the ways she interacted with herself and others.

We can't expect people to be perfect; none of us is. As we become more accepting of ourselves, we also appreciate when others are willing to expose their vulnerabilities, show their shortcomings, and admit mistakes. In doing so, we confirm that we are "cracked," and by applying the art of kintsugi with ourselves, we can heal and grow.

Exposing our vulnerabilities is an elegant way to show up more charismatically and authentically, to create more intimacy, trust, and understanding.

More Points to Prepare, Observe, and Question:

- **Be aware of your perceptions and biases:** There are two key distinctions here. One is to recognize that you have opinions and biases. The second is to ponder why you are choosing to hold on to them. So the question to you is: What are these biases? And why are you holding on to them?

- **In conversation:** When you interact with someone, what are your perceptions of them? How do you think your opinion affects your tone? What can you do differently the next time?

- **Forgiveness:** What if you were wrong about a person? What can you say to yourself that would allow you to move forward and change your relationship with that person?

- **Think for yourself:** When things don't go the right way and we fail, are these mistakes or learning moments? What makes for a learning moment?

- **Practice:** Whether at work or in a social setting, pay attention to how you view others. Just for a moment, try to adjust your perception. Do it in your next meeting or conversation. Notice what happens.

- **Staying in power:** Understand that you do not need to give up your power or position. Quite the opposite; stay in your power and stick to your high standards. People value that in you and want it from you. But focus on how you display that power. Will you be a judgmental commander or an inspiring, approachable, and admired leader?

- **Evaluate the long-term cost if things don't change. Then assess the benefit of changing:** What is the tone and language you are going to use? How will this impact the relationship?

Footnotes:

Leslie Riopel, "15 Most Interesting Self-Compassion Research Findings" (positivepsychology.com, 2021). https://positivepsychology.com/self-compassion-research

Serena Chen, "Give Yourself a Break: The Power of Self-Compassion" (*Harvard Business Review*, 2018). https://hbr.org/2018/09/give-yourself-a-break-the-power-of-self-compassion

Juliana G. Breines and Serena Chen, "Self-Compassion Increases Self-Improvement Motivation" *(Psychology Medicine,* 2012).

Kristen Neff, a self-compassion researcher, shares that people with self-compassion are less likely to be critical of themselves, anxious, or depressed, leading to greater life satisfaction. Also, Breines and Chen state that self-compassion can increase self-improvement motivation, making us more motivated to make amends and to desire not to repeat transgressions. It generates a greater desire to spend more time studying after an initial failure or a greater preference for upward social comparison after realizing a personal weakness and motivation to change it. Both of these points are helpful in understanding how important it is to use an accepting approach when it comes to personal failures.

Chapter 7

How Your Need
for Validation
Can Affect You

Learning to dance your *dance*

It was lunchtime in downtown San Francisco and I was about to present my first workshop on corporate social responsibility. The audience consisted of about fifteen friends and acquaintances who had showed up to support me. Twenty minutes in, I could feel their support slowly turning into pity. Almost everyone was painfully grimacing as they witnessed my shirt turning darker, drenched in sweat (yes, that perspiration problem you've heard about before).

Forty-five minutes later, as I thanked everyone for partici-
pating, I could hear a collective sigh of relief, as though
everyone was grateful it was finally over. "The presentation
was great," one of the participants said, "but watching you
being so nervous was excruciating." Talk about a compliment, no?

For the next two years, I took public-speaking classes
and gave presentations at every venue that would have me.
Soon I felt that I was on top of my game. But no matter
how often I presented, I continued to carry this underlying
anxiety in me.

Finally, I realized what was triggering my anxiety. My
desire to be liked and accepted made me highly critical of
my own performance, and that in turn directly affected
my ability to present comfortably and successfully.

No one wants to look like a fool, especially in front of a
large audience. However, I realized that my self-worth had
become so tied to the outcome of my presentations that it
actually derailed me from ensuring that my audience received value.

The way my anxiety affected me is far from unusual;
it's something I have witnessed numerous times with my
coaching clients and in my programs. We all get nervous,
we all get anxious, even the most ostensibly successful
among us. But we can fix this.

Henri, a director of engineering, told me in a coaching session that he doesn't feel recognized for his work and
contributions to his organization.

Ann, a product manager in a high-tech start-up, told

me about all the work she does and how much money she saves her department, but said she doesn't feel appreciated for what she does.

Mark, a data scientist, feels like his contribution to developing analytical tools isn't being recognized for its actual value, and neither are his ideas.

I have heard hundreds of stories from people who feel invisible and unappreciated. In another chapter, I'll address ways to make people feel valued; for now, let's look at how not being validated can affect someone. Then, let's explore how you can change the way you feel about yourself if you feel unappreciated and unrecognized.

In their book *Mastering Leadership,* Robert Anderson and William Adams write about the need for approval in the context of leadership effectiveness:

The more we are defined by other people's approval, the more likely we will fear rejection and be risk-averse, indecisive, cowardly, and compliant. The more we define ourselves by our results, the more likely we will fear failure and fail to delegate, collaborate, build teamwork, and allow others to engage meaningfully and creatively. We will tend to relate to others in autocratic and controlling ways. If we define ourselves on our intellectual capacity, we will fear vulnerability, fail to connect with others, fail to acknowledge their brilliance, and will relate to others in self-protecting, arrogant, analytically critical, and condescending ways.

Public speaking was a powerful trigger for my "being perfect and liked" trap. But how many times do we find ourselves in circumstances that cause the same reactions? Here are a few examples that occur frequently, particularly in positions of leadership:

- We push for perfection because perfect results will represent us in the best possible light.
- We control a process because we want to prove our worth.
- When leading a team, we are concerned about pleasing rather than following a vision.

Often, we seek short-term gratification without realizing that it can come with many long-term detriments. When we identify with our performance, we feel that our very self-worth is being attacked if we are criticized or questioned.

I believed that my performance was a representation of me as a person. So, when I feared my presentation was called into question, I felt it was *me* who was called into question. This fear created anxiety even before I had uttered a single word.

When I work with my clients on personal validation, I help them reflect on why they feel the need to be recognized. As I've said before, you can often control only how you react to events, not the events themselves. So I help them focus on the causes of these reactions first.

To help my clients, I often use the analogy of a pillar made of stones. This pillar represents who they are.

I ask, "What would it take for this pillar to stand tall and strong, unwavering and resilient, able to face a storm or strong winds?"

"It needs to be built over a foundation that is strong," they say.

"Good. What else?"

"The stones need to be placed on top of each other in a way that they fit well together, the stronger ones at the bottom, so that they can support the other stones above."

"Excellent. And what do they need to be made of?" I ask.

"Probably something strong, like granite," they answer.

I continue asking a few more questions until we understand all that is necessary to build a strong pillar that won't topple. Then I ask them to imagine this pillar as a representation of *them*. The stones represent facets of their experience and personality. I ask them to think about building their column with stones that each hold a quality of their character. If each stone has a word engraved on it, what would it say? I have them reflect on that, and often they are reluctant to say anything about themselves out loud. They'll nod and say, "OK, sure, I'll do that."

"Hmm, no. I would like to hear you say it out loud now."

They hesitate, and maybe utter something like, "I finish my projects on time," "I deliver products better than what is expected," or "I can code my way through any challenges."

"You are still not doing it," I say. "You are only describing *how* you do your work; you're not describing yourself as a *person*. What are the qualities about yourself and your character that make you work that way?"

Reluctantly, they answer, "I don't know, I guess I'm punctual."

I encourage them to say more.

"I'm smart, I'm determined to finish what I start, I'm trustworthy, I'm innovative."

You can tell they are finally describing their character once they switch to "I am" sentences, and I let them be aware of that when they do. I help them notice how difficult it is for them to use complimentary words to express their qualities. Of course, we all maintain a certain level of humility; you don't want to become a narcissistic, know-it-all braggart. But there needs to be some self-recognition for the value that you bring to people and for who you are as a person.

If you cannot see and recognize yourself for who you are, how will others be able to see those qualities in you? A healthy dose of gratitude for your contribution to the world, to your work, and to your family is hugely important.

So, in this exercise, to build your pillar, start reflecting on who you are and what you contribute. What words would you engrave on each stone? Go ahead and write some down on your list now.

Here is the key message: If you don't use the suitable stones—that is, if you don't know what qualities represent you—you always have to rely on others to identify them for you; you are building a pillar that relies on external support to stay standing. Imagine the pillar having angled bars from each side to keep it standing straight. The external anchors represent all the people from whom you continue to expect recognition and support. If you rely chiefly on them, guess what will happen if they fail to recognize you for who you are and what you provide?

I work with my clients to become more autonomous and self-sufficient, so that they realize how powerful and strong they are on their own; once they recognize their intrinsic qualities, they can function successfully without reliance on others' approval. Then, if and when they receive recognition from others, they can enjoy it that much more.

My clients have told me that, as a result of focusing on their pillar, they started showing up with more confidence, because they were not relying on others for their sense of self-worth. They noticed that their colleagues viewed them differently. Peers were drawn to them because they sensed in them more confidence and autonomy.

Natalie, a lab research technician, reported one day, "It's funny how I always used to ask others to validate my choices. Now it has shifted; people come to me and ask me for my opinion before they move forward with an idea."

Now, don't you think that is a more profound and rewarding form of recognition? Your colleagues will be able to sense when you no longer rely on external validation. Instead, they will recognize your work by asking you to do another project, asking for your help to resolve problems, or promoting you.

That is true recognition and validation.

Here are a few more tools to consider.

Remember the pitiful workshop that I opened this chapter with? My topic that day was social responsibility, and even though I was passionate about the subject, in the end it was my need for validation that prevailed. No matter how much I practiced, I continued to feel anxious and desperate to be liked. Then one day, a friend of mine asked, "Roberto, why are you doing this?"

"This what?" I said. "Presenting on social responsibility?"

"Yes, why do you want to present on this particular subject?"

"Well, because I want people to learn something new, and I want them to change for the better. I want to help them, the environment, and this world."

"Good," he said. "Then why don't you just focus on that?"

That hit me. He was right. He then added something that has stuck with me ever since:

"If you are here to serve, then serve."

If you are here to serve, then serve. This insight changed everything for me. Those few simple words transformed my beliefs. Stop thinking about what people will think of you, about whether they'll like you or not. You are here to provide something for them and that is your purpose. Just focus on your purpose and stop thinking about everything else.

Since then, I remind myself of my intention every time I start a coaching session, every time I facilitate a program, and every time I speak to an audience.

In fact, I remind myself of my purpose right now as I write the chapters of this book.

So, the questions for you are the same: Why are you doing what you are doing? What would change if you stopped thinking about what others might think and started focusing on your purpose?

The answers to both questions are often inextricably linked. When you focus on your motivation and your intent, this focus will create purpose. And purpose is what will propel you forward, mitigating your need for validation and reinforcing your pillar.

So let me share how I have built purpose for myself. I encourage you to do the same.

Listen to your calling. What are you here to do? What fills you with joy and enthusiasm?

We often believe that following our journey might disappoint others. We tend to fear failure and follow the norm because that makes us feel validated or, at least, safe. Unfortunately, if we let external recognition dictate our choices, we all lose.

Steven R. Covey calls the need for outside validation the Dependent stage of development. When we are in this stage, we want to keep everything safe, often tolerating things we shouldn't. We are afraid of losing, so we make our goals conform to safety. As you become aware of being in this dependent stage and listen to your calling, you'll be able to move to the next stage, Independence or Self-Authoring. Here is where you have to claim your pillar and *serve*.

Keep an awareness log. Recognize and take note of how you define yourself, how you engage with people, and the consequences of both. You could write down qualities you already have and those you might want to work on. For example, "I'm passionate about my work, I'm driven, I'm highly organized, I'm a natural leader, I'm an excellent communicator, I cultivate innovation, I value differences, I can handle complexities." Or, you could just add "I'm not" to these competencies and identify those that you need to cultivate more.

Another way to find your qualities is to keep track of the feedback people give you and what you learn about yourself. Then, it'll be up to you to leverage your talents and pay attention to what you need to develop. I use a similar process with clients when they need to identify competencies and shortcomings in their leadership skills, so they can then create a Development Action Plan for themselves. I've seen this work extremely well.

Keep track of the kudos. I have a kudos journal to refer to when days are tough. I realized early on that I tended to focus on the few bad reviews I received and forget about the 90 percent that were positive. It's human nature to do so, and I see this propensity toward the negative often with my clients. So I decided to keep track of my kudos and write them down. I feel no shame admitting that whenever my confidence level gets low, I read them a few times. Try it yourself and see how it affects you.

Give and enjoy giving. Practicing altruism is another way to move from being self-concerned to serving. Research has shown that the happiest people take pleasure in other people's success and show concern for others. Conversely, unhappy people find themselves deflated when their peers accomplish something noteworthy, and they often feel relieved when their colleagues fail. Research also shows that the happier the person, the less attention they pay to what others around them are doing.[5]

If you have ever volunteered or simply helped others, did you worry about what they thought of you? I doubt it.

When we offer a helping hand to someone, we are in the act of giving, and in that moment almost none of us have self-doubt. So think about how you can transfer that mindset to your work and make your purpose and intent the focus of what you do.

Be courageous in the transition. Selflessness requires that we look at the darker parts of ourselves (our shadows) and bring them to the surface.

After many years of trying to be perfect, please others, and control my world, it was hard for me to let go of what defined me. However, the exhaustion (and ruined sports coats) I experienced from maintaining that inauthentic self wasn't sustainable. I found that, in comparison, the work required to transition to a new, more authentic outlook was far less cumbersome.

In *Mastering Leadership,* Anderson and Adams write, "This transition is arduous because, to make this journey, we must let go of how we have come to define ourselves. We let go of the deeply held beliefs that our worth and value are tied up with how we are seen by

---

[5]Sonja Lyubomirsky, *The How of Happiness: A New Approach to Getting the Life You Want* (Penguin Books, 2007), 116.

others, by what we do, how smart we are, or how acceptable we are."

By eliminating the need for comparison and external input, and instead, concentrating on our values and journey toward our dreams, we can redirect our energy from the "I'll be fulfilled when . . ." mentality to "I see my worth now, and know how I can use it to help others."

As you liberate yourself from the need for approval, you'll be able to lead in far more rewarding ways.

We will later take a deeper look at recognition and praise, particularly at how important it is to praise and acknowledge others.

But wouldn't it be better if you didn't *need* affirmation as fuel for your work?

Here are a few questions for you to ponder:

- Are you relying on others' approval in order to feel impactful?

- How are your personal values affected by your hope for an expression of appreciation that may or may not come? How would you feel if you could let go of your need for validation?

- What's your calling? What is something that fills you with joy and enthusiasm?

Chapter 8

Self-Sabotage and Overcoming Your Limits

The advantage of learning new dance steps

How many times have you started something, maybe with great enthusiasm, just to see it fizzle out? How many times have you watched a conversation fall to pieces because you used counterproductive (or downright stupid) words and phrases?

Have you ever wondered why we often fail to reach our objectives?

Whether in my love life, travel, friendships, career, or business, I can remember more failures than I care to recall. It was astonishing for me to realize—after many, many years of failure and disappointment—that I was stuck in a pattern of self-sabotage.

Usually self-sabotage happens when we want something but are fearful that we won't be able to get it. Consequently, we avoid the very thing we want.

This avoidance and/or retreat is rarely a conscious process, but after repeating it for so long, avoiding and retreating become our default stance in too many situations.

We all have an upper and a lower limit, and together they set the framework within which we usually operate. When we try to achieve something that doesn't fit into this framework, because it would require us to break the constraints imposed by the lower and upper limits, we respond with fear. This fear is what compels us to get in our own way. Let's take a closer look at how this works.

Income and lifestyle provide a good example.

For me, the lower limit represents the minimum I have to earn to fulfill my basic needs. If I get too close to my lower limit, I have to work hard to stay above the lower line. I market myself, reduce my expenses, add hours to my day, or hustle to sell my services.

I have become an expert at fighting that lower threshold. Most of us are, particularly when destitution comes knocking at the door.

However, the upper limit is where we tend to sabotage ourselves. The upper limit is where we keep ourselves from earning more, living a larger life, having a higher status, finding a wonderful relationship, or getting that great job at that excellent company.

How so? The self-sabotage can take different avenues. One may simply be *Why rock the boat? Everything is going so well, you will just mess things up.* Another very common one stems from impostor syndrome, or that critical inner voice that casts doubt on our abilities, undermines our desires, and convinces us to be suspicious of ourselves or the choices we make. This voice often filled my mind with diminishing thoughts that would prevent me from achieving my goals. The fear that my inner critic generated would put me back under the covers, where I was comfortable and safe, in a familiar place with low risks. Living a low-risk life, however, also means living a life that tends to be boring and is often unaccomplished, filled with regrets. That didn't work for me.

According to Gay Hendricks in his book *The Big Leap*, the false foundation in the upper limit problem is a set of four barriers of fear:

1. Feeling Fundamentally Flawed: I cannot expand to my full creative potential because something is fundamentally wrong with me.

2. Disloyalty and Abandonment: I cannot expand to my full potential because I'd end up all alone, be disloyal to my roots, and leave people from my past behind.

3. Believing That More Success Brings a Bigger Burden: I cannot expand to my highest potential because I'd be an even bigger burden than I am now.

4. The Crime of Outshining: I must not attain my full

success because if I did, I would outshine others and make people look and/or feel bad.

As you expand your abilities, you will likely run into some or all of these barriers. Before I offer ways to overcome them, let's look at some examples that might help you recognize an upper limit and the start of self-sabotaging. Self-sabotaging behaviors can come in many different forms and are often not immediately visible. One way to check is to simply ask yourself if your behavior is actually getting you closer to your goals. You may, for example, notice behaviors like procrastination or perfectionism; these two are evident if you find yourself wasting time needing to have all the facts before you move forward. Or you may notice that you get distracted by unnecessary tasks; this frequently occurs when you create vague commitments or menial tasks, saying, "Yeah, I'll work on that next week" or "OK, maybe I can try to finish this tomorrow."

Self-sabotage is often also hidden in how we initiate and engage in conflict. Whenever you think you have good reasons to walk away from discomfort or possible shame, try looking closer. Often, we try to find problems or fault in someone else so we don't have to admit that it is we who have issues we are not ready to address. (Remember my cowardly behavior in that meeting in Chapter 1?)

In relationships, self-sabotage can stem from the fear of emotional pain and the need to protect ourselves. At work, we might be afraid to disappoint; we fear that we won't deliver what is required or feel that we don't deserve a position or project. If we are in an interview, for example, these fears can make us say all the wrong things because we secretly want to drop the ball, hoping people will turn us down.

If you sense anxiety, fear, distress, negativity, self-judgment, or the usual "I'm not good enough," these feelings could all be signs of self-sabotage. Your fears are getting in the way of your intent and inviting defeat.

Here is what distinguishes self-sabotage from genuine self-concern: when we self-sabotage, our fears are based on assumptions rather than facts. We assume we won't succeed, and so we look everywhere for validation that our assumptions of failure are correct. Consequently, and by design, we believe our failures are inevitable, and because of these beliefs, we hold ourselves back. Therefore, we must question if we have a factual basis for our assumptions. If we have no solid facts supporting them, we need to rewrite our story.

Change from negative to positive affirmations; be aware of falling back into damaging assumptions; and continuously reframe your inner dialogue to reflect a new positive story. The process of reframing your thoughts is essential in overcoming your barriers.

Now here are my suggestions for how to overcome the four barriers once you have recognized a pattern of self-sabotaging thoughts.

Overcoming Barrier One—Feeling Fundamentally Flawed

Notice if your self-sabotaging thoughts stem from old patterns or events that affected you in the past. A failed relationship, a rejection, or a poor delivery on a project can leave a mark on you, especially if you don't use a growth mindset to overcome the failures. We can't change the past, yet we can identify these sabotaging behaviors and consciously choose to counteract them.

How do we counteract self-sabotage? Well, you'll have to confront what I call the "Green Monster." At least that's the name I gave my personal saboteur. The Green Monster shows up virtually anytime I want to do something that is outside of my comfort zone.

The GM opens his big mouth and says, "C'mon, Roberto, why do you want to do this new thing, what do you have to prove to yourself? Just relax, sit here on the sofa and watch a movie." I am sure you have your own version of the Green Monster.

What I found works for me is to "talk" to my GM. I'll have a serious tête-à-tête to get things straight. I've spoken to him so many times that by now my GM has become my friend.

If I know he is trying to hold me back because of unfounded fears and to convince me to stay in the no-risk zone, I ask him to evaluate the current conditions and possible positive outcomes. Together we list the pros and cons, sorting out assumptions and facts.

I'm not always in a mood to talk though, and when I am not, I simply ask him to leave me alone. I push him away, because now is not the time, now is my time to shine and to try something new. It's OK if I fail, but I need to move forward because living in regret is not an option.

To help you redirect your thoughts when the Green Monster shows up, explore these questions:

- What will happen if you keep things the way they are?

- What is the potential impact of changing the way you work/live/eat/exercise, etc.?

- How much longer do you want to put up with current circumstances?

Overcoming Barrier Two—Disloyalty and Abandonment

Ah, this one was also something I experienced—the fear that if I got to be successful, it would take me away from my loved ones. I'd be alone and unfaithful to my roots. Being away would mean being disloyal to my family, friends, and the culture in which I grew up. I wouldn't be present to support them and celebrate their lives.

I remember the pressure I felt from my parents when I left Europe to establish myself in the United States. I wanted to create a new life for myself and do something important. In addition to that, I sometimes felt guilt and grief from being separated from the people closest to me. As a result, at times I was holding back from expanding my life in the Bay Area and sabotaging my professional growth because I wasn't sure if I should stay. My Green Monster was pointing fingers at me for leaving my roots and saying, "If you stay here, you'll end up all alone, and you are disloyal to your roots."

Over time, I discovered that, although I was living across the ocean, I wouldn't be where I was if I didn't feel the love and support of my distant family. I was able to operate efficiently in the U.S. *because* of their unquestionable love. I realized that, although far away, I was never completely alone or abandoned.

Not only did I have strong ties to my roots, but because of their love, I also built another family here. I created friendships with people who were in similar circumstances, and I realized that I was not alone or disloyal—quite the opposite.

These GM-like saboteurs often stem from the stories we create and from the concepts we project upon others. I would advise you to challenge both your stories and your projections by communicating with the people you believe you are disloyal to, and speaking openly with your family and friends. Be open to learning that they may feel differently from what you imagined.

Ironically, you may even find that they could be the ones telling you to move away and start living your life independently. Also, if they are not supportive of you and your endeavors, you might want to reevaluate these relationships.

Overcoming Barrier Three—Believing That More Success Brings a Bigger Burden

This one is tricky.

We can be so accustomed to our comfortable life and habits that we fear success will disrupt it all. We are afraid of upsetting a comfortable job that is easy and provides a healthy paycheck. So while we wish for a higher position, higher income, and more success, we sabotage ourselves because we are afraid that success will disrupt the life we have and know. Even the failures that keep us in our current conditions have become comfortable, and we accept them as part of our lives or careers. Therefore, success can represent a complete transformation of our life, a major transition into something that we perceive as horribly unfamiliar, even a threat.

For example, let's say you desire a new project that could move you up in your organization. Yet when you realize there are no possibilities for you to advance, you are secretly relieved because you won't need to experience uncomfortable change. So you get a short reprieve from avoiding these changes and fall back into the comfortable but stagnant life you know.

I've coached people who hoped they would be turned down for a speaking engagement because they were afraid of addressing a large audience, even though they had worked for months on this opportunity and knew that it could easily catapult their business. I've had clients tell me they didn't return phone calls from potential customers because they feared they wouldn't be good enough to do the job (even when those customers reached out to them because they believed my clients were the best in their field). My clients were afraid that if these opportunities materialized and were successful, their lives would change drastically.

Fortunately, there is a powerful way to address this barrier. Simply put, you can look at your success as a burden, or you can think about it with less attachment by staying in the flow. What does that mean? Well, it requires a shift in how you view success. It requires looking at the new job, the speaking engagement, or the new clients as openings into a new world that you can manage at your own pace—not as objects of intimidation.

Whenever such an opening presents itself, it offers you the possibility to launch into new opportunities. It nudges you to take small steps to overcome the upper limit. Don't immediately reject the offers; it's normal to feel overwhelmed when you first get an assignment. Take a moment, breathe, discuss it with someone, and see how the first fearful reaction may dissipate.

When you get these opportunities, it doesn't mean you cannot find a suitable pace so as not to get overwhelmed. When you fill up your fridge with fresh groceries, every time you open that door, do you feel overwhelmed and say, "Oh my God, all that food. I'll never be able to eat it!"? Of course not; after a week of breakfast, lunch, and dinner, it's all gone.

Trust that everything will fall into place to help you along the way. And don't forget that you are still in charge, and you can manage the goals one step at a time, at your own pace. Slowly, you'll find yourself in a better position and still be able to enjoy your life.

Overcoming Barrier Four—The Crime of Outshining

For this one, I'll start with the poem "Our Deepest Fear," by Marianne Williamson: "Our deepest fear is not that we are inadequate./ Our deepest fear is that we are powerful beyond measure./ It is our light, not our darkness/ that most frightens us . . . . . . Your playing small/ does not serve the world./ There is nothing enlightened about shrinking/ So that other people won't feel insecure around you./ We are all meant to shine,/ As children do . . . It's not just in some of us;/ It is in everyone./ And as we let our own light shine,/ We unconsciously give other people permission to do the same./ As we are liberated from our own fear,/ Our presence automatically liberates others."

I've seen people sabotage their success because of guilt. I had a client who told me, "If I'm successful and make a lot of money, I feel like I'm moving into a world of privilege, and it's not fair to those who are suffering." I understood that reaction because I used to think the same way earlier in my life. But then someone said, "Roberto, what if you became successful and earned more money, and were able to help the people who need it most? Wouldn't that be an even better privilege?" That changed my mind. Before, I was so stuck in my guilt that I failed to realize how I was limiting my growth and with it my ability to help the causes or people I cared about.

Keep expanding and shining your light. Remain connected to your roots and the important objectives you have, and then decide how you'll support others with your generosity.

Now, as you think about yourself—what you want to achieve and who you want to be—how are you sabotaging your progress? It took me a very long time to overcome these barriers because I didn't have someone to help me with my saboteurs. But over the years, I've learned to be more aware of my self-defeating thoughts. I took the time to understand the fear behind my saboteurs, then I worked my way forward. As I did that, my barriers dissipated.

In summary, we are often familiar with the lower limit

because of the friction it creates. When we are afraid we might not be able to provide for our most basic needs, we tend to fight against our lower limit and push away from it with incredible force. The upper limit, however, is less tangible and less visible. Yet, if we are to keep our dreams and visions alive, we must work just as hard at overcoming these barriers.

We are built for change, and we have an endless, innate drive to achieve. It is in our human nature. So we may as well learn how to deal with that upper threshold. Not making a decision, and thereby allowing our saboteurs to take control, is the same as deciding to do nothing.

Questions:

- Have you noticed patterns of self-sabotage in your work, relationships, or goals?

- Look back on your life and reflect on times when you allowed a dream to crumble. Were you reaching your upper limit?

- What is a vision that will inspire you and give you the courage to shatter that upper limit so you can create a new, higher, yet still comfortable normal?

Part 2

Dancing with Others

The password to dancing with others is *empathy*.

Just as you can adapt your product or system to a target audience, so can you adapt your attitude, language, and behavior to the people you interact with. Remember that they are, in fact, people, with concerns, emotions, and fears. Their lives beyond the workplace are often complicated.

Just as you need to be present, mindful, and receptive with a partner on the dance floor, you need to truly listen to and create rapport with your team and coworkers.

Listening requires empathy. Without empathy, you will neither achieve your career objectives nor manage to do "the dance."

With higher levels of empathy, you will create more rewarding and trusting connections, empower your team members, and increase your business performance. As a result, you will be recognized as a true leader in your field.

Chapter 9

Mind Your Language

*Pay attention to how
you are dancing*

When I was in my twenties, I took a four-month backpacking trip through Southeast Asia. Near the end, I boarded a plane in Kathmandu, Nepal, and flew over the Himalayas to Lhasa, in Tibet, where my travel companions and I spent the next four days. We decided to return to Kathmandu by land and began the journey with a nine-hour bus ride from Lhasa to Shigatse. The road was one of the bumpiest and dustiest I had ever been on, and it gave me a whole new interpretation of what a "pain in the ass" means.

On the second day, we hitchhiked a ride on a truck. We sat outside on the open cargo bed, crossing over 15,000-foot mountain passes. We were wearing every last shred of clothing we had just to keep warm; still, I was shivering for hours. A little before sunset, we pulled into a truck stop to spend the night. The large room had no heating, and I woke up in the morning with a fever.

The next day, we were back on the same truck for a twelve-hour ride to Zhangmu, a port of entry into Nepal. I was sick and tired. By the time I arrived, all I could do was eat a bowl of soup and go to bed.

The next morning I woke up and decided to walk to the border, which was only a few hundred yards below my hotel. It was 8:30 a.m. Local people were sitting on a short wall, smoking cigarettes and eating pastries. I didn't know what they were waiting for, nor did I care. There was a small walkway bridge over the main road by the outpost. I didn't see any gates or barriers, just a few signs, in unreadable Chinese, and none of the typical large red stop signs. I looked around and inside the building at the foot of the bridge. I called out for somebody, but I got no response. There was no one there, I thought, and so I proceeded across the border.

I had barely crossed through when I heard a man yelling at me from the top of the overpass. I couldn't understand anything he said, but he gesticulated for me to turn around and come back up. I obeyed. As I got closer, he kept yelling, pushing me inside the main room. He grabbed my backpack and threw it in the middle of the floor. I had no idea what was going on.

Then he aimed his machine gun at me, and I saw him racking the charging handle on its right side. Not good, I thought, not good at all. He loaded it.

I've seen such things in movies many times, but I'd never had a machine gun pointed at me. Plus, I was still feverishly ill. And this man was clearly angry. He kept yelling, and I kept not understanding a word. By then, my mind was racing and my heart pounding, my mouth and eyes were wide open. I knew I had to deescalate the situation immediately. But how? How could I communicate without knowing the language?

That moment was a defining one for me, as it taught me that just as critical as our language is, our expressions, attitude, and mindset play as big a role in conveying an impression and communicating a message.

The first thing I did was raise my hands about chest height and make a placating up-and-down motion. The guard continued to yell at me. I then proceeded to explain to him, with hand gestures and my voice, that I had walked by (walking fingers) and looked inside (pointing at my eyes and then out and around), that I had called for someone (mimicking looking around with big eyes and saying "hello, hello") and then listened for someone (cupped hand behind my ear and big eyes looking). I then made that face you make when you throw your hands in the air and somehow express, "I don't know, go figure," and did the walking fingers again, to show how I had just kept walking. All the while, my heartrate was easily up to 140. For the first time in my life, I thought I might piss myself from fear.

The guy made some adjustments to his machine gun and lowered it. His body showed that he recognized I had been—and probably still was—just an idiot and not ill-intentioned. (Maybe he had also been afraid that his superior would chew him out for leaving his post and letting me "sneak" across the border.)

In any case, he then pointed to 9:00 a.m. on a large clock on the wall, as though telling me when the place opened, and asked me to wait until then. He grabbed the backpack from the floor and helped me put it back on. I walked out of the building and up the road, unzipping my coat to dry all the sweat. Head down, I approached the other locals and sat on the wall with them, my feet dangling, my nervous system still racing.

I should have just gotten a pastry, I thought. These people have no idea what I've just been through.

What I understood that day is something many of us have experienced: when in a dire situation, we may have to rely on our most basic means of communication.

For me, that moment of fear and stress made me realize the importance of paying attention to every gesture, expression, tone of voice, and attitude in relating to others. This was a moment when I couldn't afford to make a mistake. I had only a rudimentary knowledge of gestures (though lots of practice as an Italian), but I had an intuitive understanding of the importance of nonverbal communication. Many studies have shown that if you only listen to what a person says and ignore what their expressions and body language tell you, you'll only know half the story. Similarly, if you are not aware of how your emotions affect the way you show up in conversations and of the message that your facial expressions and gestures send, you can only get so far in building rapport.

Several years ago, I saw a documentary about an experiment that demonstrated how a seemingly insignificant detail could create an entirely different outcome in people's perceptions.

The experiment took place in a store. When customers paid for their items, the cashier was asked to faintly touch the customer's hand as they exchanged the receipt or payment. The cashiers would do this to half the shoppers; the other half would not receive any physical contact.

As the customers walked out of the store, someone would ask their opinion about the cashier and the quality of the service received. And here is the interesting part: when the worker touched the customers' hands, the shoppers gave positive feedback; when the worker did not touch their hands, the opinion was neutral to negative. This shows that even the smallest physical touches (e.g., a simple pat on the back to acknowledge a job well done) can have an enormous influence on how we interface with one another. Now, consider the impact of adjusting your tone of voice, your facial expression, or your choice of words.

Back at the Chinese border, the consequences of my behavior could have been entirely different had I conveyed self-righteous anger or indignation. It wasn't the gestures alone that saved me, it was the human interaction.

You are communicating with your whole body—your eyes, your tone of voice, how you carry yourself. If you are sensitive to how you interact with others, both verbally and nonverbally, you will be amazed at how much more others can comprehend you and, consequently, trust you. Even if your communication fails, at least your audience will trust that you are trying to communicate better with them.

Every interaction offers you an opportunity to fine-tune your art of communication.

I am not only talking about relating facts and data; that's only one side of communication. I've seen technical engineers, data scientists, and surgeons who were brilliant in conveying even the most complex concepts. They could talk about linear regression, hyperparameters, gradient descent, or shapely curves. What made their talks so convincing was the fact that they used a language that was adapted perfectly to their audience. "Adapted" does not mean that they were speaking inauthentically in any way; they just knew how to use terminology their audience could relate to.

Now, apply this principle of adaptation to other types of communication, where you also modify your attitude, expressions, and tone of voice. Doing so will enable others to not just relate to data but to *you*.

When you understand and know how to navigate both your nonverbal skills and your verbal communication, not only will your technical abilities be appreciated but also who you are as a person.

This comprehensive communication will allow you to better showcase your ideas and gain traction in your organization. If your coworkers understand your data but not your ability to lead, inspire, or influence, how will they be able to see you for all you are?

Key to improving communication is to become aware

of the dissonance between how you think you communicate and how others perceive your communication. So before we delve deeper here, let's take a look at some common behaviors we use to protect ourselves.

I have been (and sometimes, still am) guilty of most of the below (adapted from Mark Goulston).[6]

What You Think You Are	How You Might Be Perceived
Confident	Arrogant, condescending, cocky
Astute	Sly, dishonest
Humorous	Inappropriate, improper, tasteless
Passionate	Impulsive, abrupt
Someone with great ideas	Opinionated, judgmental
Strong	Rigid, uncompromising
Detail-oriented	Fussy, nitpicky, aversive to decisive action
Sensitive	Needy, easily upset, defensive
Quiet	Passive, tolerant, indecisive
Energetic	Hyperactive, scattered

As you can see, how others interpret your outward, public self can be quite different from the self you think you are projecting. If you are unaware of the discrepancy, you are bound to sabotage your relationships.

If you are not sure about how you are perceived, an excellent way to find out is to ask your close friends or co-workers. You could do a simple anonymous survey or ask them directly to give you an honest answer.

Here is a simple exercise I have done in classrooms, and participants have received the most interesting responses. Grab your phone and send a text message to people who

---

[6] Mark Goulston, *Just Listen: Discover the Secret to Getting Through to Absolutely Anyone* (AMACOM, 2015), 80.

know you well. Give them a few hours to answer and ask them to tell you the first thing that comes to mind, with honesty, based on these three questions:

1. What have you noticed is my default reaction or behavior when I am under stress?
2. How do I show up, and what is my behavior, when someone or something challenges my values?
3. How do I show up when I am in a happy place in my life, and how does it affect the people around me?

They could reply to you with a few keywords for each question—no need to give lengthy explanations. Then compare their responses to your thoughts about your attitude. This will help you be more conscious of what you bring to the table, so you can better anticipate your reactions.

As you receive their answers, notice what is happening to you. Do the responses surprise you? In what contexts or conversations do you remember appearing this way or that way?

When I ask these questions to my clients, they often know the answers. They say something like, "You know, I sensed something was odd about that conversation" or "I was wondering why I hadn't heard back from her since we talked" or "I sensed discomfort right after I said that." For me personally, I could usually tell when I said the wrong thing because I felt a rush of heat or I blushed in embarrassment. If we take a pause and recognize what we are sensing (which is often uneasiness), we'll realize when we have "crossed the line" in the past. You will see that your friends' responses were honest and you need to honestly reckon with them.

When you find yourself standing on the other side of that line, you'll need to (1) Reflect on what brought you there. Is it something you said or failed to address? Did you have the wrong attitude or any biases before your conversation? What caused you to fall into this predicament? As you reflect on what happened, you'll then need to (2) Acknowledge that there could be areas of yourself and your behavior that may need some adjustment.

There is an easy way to know when you have accomplished the first step (Reflect): if you have, you will sense the second part (Acknowledge) in your gut. It will be uncomfortable and you may even feel humiliated for your past behavior. However, if you have the courage to face your faults and maybe even apologize to others, it's ultimately not shame but a sense of achievement that will prevail.

Finally, it is just as important to recognize the answers to the third question you asked your friends and coworkers. The times you have communicated in empathetic and friendly ways say a lot about you, too. We would do ourselves a disservice if we only focused on our flaws and mistakes. It is at least as crucial to understand what is working well.

When I'm sharing my methods to create rapport, it's because I've paid attention and noticed what works for me. You, as well, need to recognize the different ways you connect with others. What are the unique, charismatic ways that have worked for you? Leverage these and use them to create rapport. I guarantee you that it will bring more collaboration and camaraderie.

Change is always in the moment. The way you see yourself and who you want to be is created—or destroyed—in moments of courage and moments of aggravation, in awareness or obliviousness. I had to muster what little courage I had (and it wasn't much, folks) to not lose control when that Chinese guard racked his machine gun and pointed it at me.

You are going to fail again and again; Lord knows I still do. But it's what you do with your failures that counts. You have the power to own your mistakes and work through them until they're resolved. You've done this a million times with all your equations and programs; you can apply the same process to yourself.

And don't be hard on yourself when you realize you could have done better. From every experience, there is something good to learn. Finding that silver lining is what allows you to move on. If you want to remain stuck in the same dilemma, feeling resentful and victimized, be my guest, and good luck. If, however, you want to get over it, you must forgive yourself, be grateful for the learning, look for the next opportunity, and move on.

Imagine yourself at a border crossing. Except you won't be walking across a border line but reaching out across a conference room table. Nobody is pointing a gun at you; still, you may feel that you are under the gun. You need to achieve your goals, and for that you will have to adapt your attitude, language, and behavior to the audience to create the rapport you need.

Questions:

- Are you aware of how you show up in conversations (your tone of voice, posture, body language, and the impression you give)?

- How do people perceive you in general? Take some time to reflect on the table from Mark Goulston. Can you think of times when your self-perception differed from how others perceived you?

- What adjustments do you believe you should make?

Chapter 10

Countersteering and the Art of Listening

Let your partner lead

W hen we meet influential people, they often seem to have a presence about them that is so strong that it radiates from them. When they interact with others, they are focused and committed to the person and the interaction. They are, in a word, fully present. To be right there, open, and attentive, is the most powerful—and the most gracious—way to connect with your audience. And all it really requires is one crucial skill: to listen, to truly listen.

The most common misunderstanding about motorcycles revolves around how to take a turn. Unlike cars, where you have to turn your steering wheel to the right or left to change direction, with motorcycles, you lean into the curve by first "countersteering." Yes, as weird as it may sound, you do a quick steer to the left to turn right. If you like scientific explanations, here is one for you:

Countersteering is both an input and an output achieved by employing push steering and is the first step in the leaning and cornering process. You push on the right grip to go right, on the left grip to go left. In a right turn, countersteering happens when gravity and gyroscopic forces momentarily push the front wheel off toward the left, which forces the bike to lean toward the right. The rider and the bike lean around the center of mass. To turn, the rider steers the front wheel off in a slight tangent, which shifts the contact patch away from the turn, forcing the top of the bike to lean toward the turn.[7]

Got it? I knew you would. And for the rest of you whose eyes have glazed over, imagine getting the feet kicked out from under you; your feet go one way but your body falls the opposite way. There are other forces at play on a motorcycle, but that is the basic explanation of turning.

A beginning rider's first goal is to stay upright. Once this is achieved, riders must learn to maintain their balance in the turns. If they go too slow and try to lean too much, they fall over. Go too fast, and they are pushed out of the

---

[7]"The Force Behind How a Motorcycle Leans," www.eatsleepride.com.

curve. If they lean on the wrong side, not in alignment with the motorcycle and the turn, they lose control and crash. It's only by leaning into the curve, their body aligned with the bike at the right speed, that all flows well.

Seem complicated? It really isn't; if you ride a bicycle, ski, or snowboard, you are already unconsciously using some of these principles: leaning in, aligning, and being in the flow.

When you enter a dialogue—any dialogue, really—you want to apply the exact same principles. Let's say you need to address some issues with a team member. You know that his or her reaction is ultimately out of your control, but if you let go of the need for control, if you countersteer and lean in by choosing a mental state that makes your body language, words, and behavior flow together and in alignment with the person you are addressing, you will present yourself in a charismatic and caring way. Choosing who you want to be in this conversation is entirely in your control. The first and most important skill is to be present. To see what that looks like, let's get back on the metaphorical motorcycle.

I always tell people that riding a motorcycle is the best and fastest way to understand what it means to be present and mindful. The reason you have to be present is that you have no other choice. If you are distracted, not focused on the road, and not quick to react, you can get yourself (and others) into big trouble. If you don't notice the bits of gravel or the pothole in the road, the wet patches or the oil spills, if you are not aware of the million things that can surprise you at any time, you are in serious danger.

Being present on a motorcycle is not just about awareness of external dangers, you also need to be mindful of your thoughts and sensations. You must not let your mind wander off, worrying about, say, work or judging other drivers (I know the latter is not an easy one). Only if you remain focused, mindful, and present at all times are you safe.

Charismatic people are mindful and in the moment. They are aware of their surroundings, of what is happening in front of them, and they are focused on the person they are interacting with.

A charismatic person listens with intention.

Maybe you already think of yourself as a good listener, maybe you feel you've got this one. If so, I would like to ask you to be open to changing your idea of what listening is all about and how it's markedly different from merely hearing. I've practiced and taught a variety of methods, but I think each one of them can be boiled down to three different stages:

1) **About you:** In this stage, your focus is mostly on yourself; even the way you listen is all about you. Instead of listening to the other person, your mind is running into every possible corner to find solutions. You are listening to the voices in your head and can't wait to share your viewpoint. STOP! This is the most aggravating thing you can do, and you don't even realize how detrimental it is to your relationships. You are not present, and it shows in your face, eyes, attitude, and energy. The other person

can tell you are not paying attention, and this will anger them.

Why? Primarily, if your listening is about you, the other person will get the feeling that what they have to say doesn't matter; you are making them feel irrelevant. Stop kidding yourself if you think people don't notice your lack of attention.

Now, here is the way to change the way you listen: make it about *them*.

2) **About them:** Here is where you start paying attention to the other person. You are fully present, with no distractions, and you quiet your mind to be entirely focused on them and what they are sharing with you. You are now in a space that is defined more by your curiosity than your need to offer answers. In "curiosity mode," you will be able to discover and learn about the other person and you will, most likely, discover something new. When you are truly listening to someone, you also reflect on what you are hearing and ask questions to understand better. You pay attention not only to what people say but also to their tone of voice and posture. You allow yourself to be fully open to the other person.

At this stage, you have to learn to be comfortable with silence, to take a breath and relax into the conversation without feeling the need to "jump in" all the time. This isn't a radio show; you can allow for "dead air" and be patient with the silence. Be a sponge, be mindfully engaged, and speak only to ask questions or to bring clarity.

While listening, be sure to validate what you hear. You can acknowledge with a simple nod, a compassionate expression, or with phrases like, "I hear you, "This is interesting," "Good point," or "I can tell you are disappointed, angry, concerned," and then remain silent and see what unfolds.

If you listen well, you'll get immediate feedback that you are appreciated and that you are making the other person feel heard. Observe how people relax into the conversation. Often, they stop speaking fast, they complain less, and they soften their posture. You will notice how the tone of their voice changes and how their body moves from a forward position to leaning back. Now this person feels *seen*. If you prioritize seeing people, they will more likely see you as someone they can trust. When you sense that connection, it's like plugging into each other and listening to music in unison.

3) **About sensing everything:** Here you are in an even higher state of presence, where you listen with all your senses. Here you are sensing the energy in the room, you hear the words behind the words, and you feel what the person is sharing. You get an idea of what is happening from facial expressions. You are paying attention to body language, tone of voice, and energy. As your curiosity deepens, you follow your gut feeling and ask open-ended questions to validate what you are sensing, such as, "I'm sensing frustration. What is happening right now? or "It feels like something is not right. What is

missing here?" or "I'm sensing pushback. What else do we need to talk about?"

Asking questions like the above shows that you are aware of and empathetic toward the other person. Your inquiries show that you care and are willing to hear their point of view. Your speaker will feel less alone, and, consequently, less anxious, less afraid, and more connected.

Research by Guy Itzchakov and Avi Kluger[8] has shown that speakers who feel listened to report higher self-awareness, lower anxiety, and greater clarity around their attitudes; when they interact with distracted listeners, they report the opposite. The speakers were also able to think more holistically and envision solutions to a higher degree. Thus, the research demonstrated that attentive, empathetic listening encouraged speakers to feel relaxed, be more self-aware, and be more capable of reflection.

Most problems you have in your workplace and in your relationships can be resolved simply by listening better. Trust me, I am an authority on this. I used to be an expert in horrible listening, especially in my younger years. Countless times, I was driven by my emotions and my controlling attitude, and I didn't allow space for listening and paying attention to others. I've messed up in my work, in relationships with friends and colleagues, in my family, and in my marriage. I've replayed these failures in my head many times, often with deep regrets, and whenever appropriate, I have apologized.

So, if you not only want to improve your relationships

---

[8]Guy Itzchakov and Avi Kluger, "The Power of Listening in Helping People Change" (*Harvard Business Review*, 2018).

but also become a more powerful influencer and charismatic person, start by paying attention to how you listen.

I love the Chinese character for the word "listening." The symbol includes different elements required to listen:

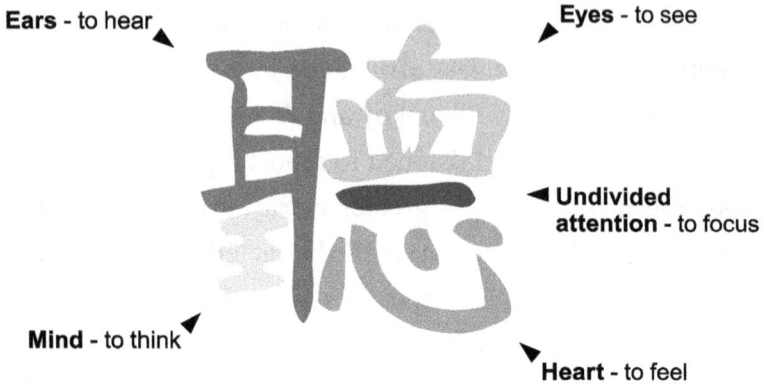

Ears - to hear ◣   ◤ Eyes - to see

聽

◀ Undivided
attention - to focus

Mind - to think ◥

▼
Heart - to feel

1. At the top are the **Ears** and **Eyes**, to hear and see the other person.

2. Then the **Mind**, to think about the words and ideas shared.

3. Next the **Undivided attention** and focus to be present in the moment.

4. Finally the **Heart**, to feel and sense what's happening and empathize with the speaker.

There is no better symbol, in my view, to explain how these five elements need to work together.

Are you truly committed to becoming a great listener and charismatic influencer? If so, here are the next steps that will get you there.

Set aside your biases. In my coaching sessions and classes, I often mention biases after sharing a model for how to give difficult feedback. If you enter a discussion with preconceived notions about the other person, guess what? No matter what you say, your energy won't reflect your words, and the people you talk to will sense that incongruity. So, as you listen to the other person, quiet your mind, let your biases fade into the background, and open yourself up to seeing their side of the world.

Set an intention to not interrupt, no matter what. Let people talk and share. Relax your facial muscles, don't frown, show up open-minded, and be receptive. I know it can be hard, but you're going to have to practice biting your tongue and trying to understand what the other person is saying before leaping in with your "answer."

Remember what I said about people talking to the lamppost?

Be curious. If you listen well, inevitably more thoughts and questions will come up. As you move into curiosity mode, you'll ask open-ended questions about the speakers, their stories, and what is happening in their lives. As you listen, more and more questions will come up, and not only will you gain more information, you'll also bring the speakers to a place of self-reflection and insight.

Repeat and rephrase what you heard. It's a form of acknowledgment, understanding, and validation of their experience. If you are not certain about something they said, you can say, "I'm trying to get a sense of what you're feeling, and I think it's XYZ. Is this correct?" Let the person either agree with you or correct you.

Then ask them, "How frustrated, angry, tired (or other emotion) are you?" Or, more directly, "How is this issue affecting you?" Again, give them time to respond. Be prepared for a cascade of emotions. A lot might come out as you allow them to share. Listen, hold back judgments, and don't respond, even if you disagree, until they have finished. Let them vent, and they'll help you learn.

Acknowledge the struggle. Say something like, "It must be challenging to go through this work. No wonder you feel frustrated, tired, etc." Use your own words, be genuine, and mean it. Acknowledging the speaker's struggle is key because it will make him or her feel heard and understood. They know that you have their back, and that will help them to finally let go of all the weight and stress. A tip: when you acknowledge, don't say, "I understand," but rather "That's understandable." Keep it neutral; after all, you are not in their shoes and can't fully understand.

Support them moving forward. If you believe that the person you are talking to would benefit from your support, ask how you can help them. Here is when you move someone toward a solution by helping them discover how to initiate change. You'll know quickly if a person just wants to share a story or actually needs your help working through a problem. Adjust your questions accordingly and help them find their own solutions.

Know that the words "I know what you mean" don't necessarily mean "I agree with you." These words only show that you are willing to listen to them, their perspective, and their struggles. By showing that you understand them, you keep the door open, and they will recognize that, even if you disagree, you are allowing future conversations to happen.

Follow through on your conversations with actions. If you agree on next steps and commitments, then both of you need to stick to what you agreed on and check in regularly for progress reports. If there is no final commitment, don't worry; the other person will let you know when they are ready to talk again. If you were a good listener, I guarantee you that they will reach out again. It would change the world if everyone just practiced mindful listening, no?

Now, when you are in your next meeting, one-on-one conversation, or just a simple chat with a friend, start by paying attention to how you listen. It's all right if you slip into old habits, but keep reflecting on how present you are.

- Were you able to quiet your mind, stay focused, and stop being distracted?
- Were you curious?
- Did you learn something from the speaker because you allowed the space for reflection?
- Did you ask questions? (At a minimum, you should ask five questions over the course of the conversation.)
- Did you validate the other person's points of view?
- What was the energy like?
- At which of the three stages were you listening?
- How much of the time did you talk versus listen? (In a work meeting, if you are the leader, good practice should be 80 percent listening, 20 percent talking.)
- What could you do differently next time?

Chapter 11

To Be as Free as Giuseppe

Be a responsive dance partner

G iuseppe, my eleven-year-old cousin, made me realize how simple and enjoyable relationships can be when no filters cloud our perceptions.

In the summer of 2017, while sitting outside a gelateria near my hometown in Puglia, Italy, my relatives asked me about my work as a coach. Giuseppe was listening to our conversation. With a curious look on his face, he asked, *"Ma Roberto, cosa fa un coach?"* ("But Roberto, what does a coach do?")

I tried the standard answer: "We help people reach their

goals and overcome obstacles by asking provocative questions, so they can find their own solutions to achieve their objectives." By the look on his face, I could tell my answer wasn't satisfying. So, I offered to show him how it worked by coaching him on the spot.

I asked him, "How about you tell me what you would like to achieve in the near future?"

He thought about it for a moment and said, "I would like to learn how to play tennis."

"OK, so what will it take for you to reach that goal?"

"Well, I first need a tennis racket and tennis balls."

"Very good. How can you get those things?" I asked.

"I need to go to the store to buy them."

"And how will you buy them?"

"I have some savings." (I could tell he was proud of that, so I nodded approvingly.)

"Perfect! What else do you need?"

He thought for a minute and then said, "I think I should probably take some lessons."

"Great. And where can you get lessons?"

"There's a tennis court not far from here. I can ask them for lessons."

"And how will you pay for the lessons?"

"Hmm, that's more difficult," he said, then he looked up at his dad, seeking approval. "Maybe I can ask my dad for help or take more money out of my savings?"

"OK, and where is the tennis court?"

"It's a few miles away. I could ask my mom to drive me there." His mom smiled and seemed to approve.

"Great, so when will you start doing all this?"

"I think the tennis lessons will start in September. I can prepare during the summer."

"Excellent! That's it. I just coached you to achieve your goal. We'll add a dash of accountability, and you're on your way."

He looked at me, stunned, and said, "Hmm, OK. I kinda see how this works."

Then he turned to his parents and said, "So, am I taking tennis lessons, then?"

We continued savoring our gelatos and enjoying the evening breeze.

The next day, I woke up thinking about how smooth and straightforward that coaching interaction had been. I was amazed by the ease with which my little cousin moved from one step to another with autonomy and free of personal bias, self-doubt, or limitations. Of course, Giuseppe has been very fortunate to grow up in a loving family, and not every teenager has that chance. It made me think about how, as we age, we are exposed to so many social experiences that affect our perceptions and beliefs, and therefore, our attitude and how we express ourselves.

The questions I asked Giuseppe, had they been posed to an adult, might have revealed a host of concerns, such as *What if I don't play well? What are people going to think of me? Who am I to think I can play tennis?* and *I'm too old, slow, fat, thin, lazy, insecure, and stiff to play.* Whenever we initiate change, we find ourselves confronted with a series of doubts and fears; I call them my gremlins. Our gremlins tend to be heavy weights on our shoulders, heavy enough to delay or even stunt our progress.

In the past few years, I've noticed that most of my clients react in one of three ways when under stress, i.e., when a gremlin shows up: **Retreat, Fight,** or **Cope.**

Retreat: Thoughts of being a victim dominate this primary reaction mode. We feel a lack of control over the outcomes in our life, and we are affected by the events, beliefs, and perceptions that hold us back from success. We have a low level of inspiration and give up easily. Operating in this mode limits us from seeing opportunities or believing that they can be realized. The victim mindset is draining and often imparts a heavy mental, emotional, and physical toll on us and the people around us.

Fight: This reaction involves anger, resentment, and defiance. In this mode, we fight back for control. We focus on everything that's wrong and feel unappreciated. We operate by force or coercion; we can be bossy or condescending, and want to micromanage rather than lead. The fight (or control) attitude can be effective in the short term, but over time it will become exhausting and aggravating. Equally important, it tends to alienate others and make them dissatisfied and unproductive.

Cope: The keywords here are *rationalization* and *toleration*. People who cope will motivate themselves by finding ways to forgive, compromise, and explain away resentment or stress, to encourage cooperation and productivity. Someone in coping mode may respond with phrases like "I'm fine" or "It's OK" to maintain harmony and the status quo. Here, by being passive and disinterested, people don't honor their values and needs. Consequently, they most likely live a mediocre and unfulfilled life or career and are not much fun to be around.

There is nothing wrong with having any of the above responses, especially under stress. I've often reacted in these modes as well. But, as you can imagine, such responses will sooner or later harm your life and career if you fail to recognize them and work on them. Going through a divorce or a loss in your life can take a while to get over; that's normal. Ruminating over a missed deadline, a bug in your code, or a prospect not calling you back, however, is unproductive and a hindrance to your performance.

I wish we could all turn back the clock and be more like Giuseppe, lighthearted and free of self-doubt, just picking a goal and going for it. But that is not the case; so, now what? Life will put all sorts of hindrances in our way that affect our perceptions, how we view ourselves, and our approach to our goals. Left unchecked, these hindrances will accumulate and eventually build up to what I call "the mud." However, we don't need to stay stuck in this goo. There are ways to begin to dilute it and eliminate it entirely, namely:

Check in with yourself. Take time during your day to evaluate your emotional state. Ask yourself, In which mode am I operating right now? Do I feel sorry for myself (Retreat)? Am I sensing anger, resentment, or the need to control (Fight)? Am I tolerating something that's harmful, am I not caring enough, or am I disengaged (Cope)?

Turn on your discomfort detector. When I ask a question of a coaching client that touches on a sensitive point, I can easily detect discomfort in them. There is a sudden change in their tone, a higher pitch, a rattling in the throat—they are under stress.

I know you are capable of noticing these fluctuations in yourself. Think about times when your voice changed because you were embarrassed or in an awkward situation. Your throat tightened, you may have blushed, or you couldn't find the right words. I've experienced countless awkward moments like this. My personal clues are voice changes and "self-combustion." What's great about these uncomfortable moments is that when you recognize them in yourself, you'll be more aware of them in others.

Put a label on it. Once you determine what and how you feel, call it out, just as you would with someone you love and trust. Be playful about it (e.g., "Here I am, downplaying my values again and not caring.") Once you put a playful spin on your reaction, you'll lighten up the mood and gain clarity. Then kick yourself back into shape or do something to break the pattern. Here again, you can say something out loud, like "Nope, not this time. I'm not going to be a victim. I'll pick up the phone and make three more sales calls today."

Ask for feedback. Another way to recognize your mode is to receive input from people around you. You can get this feedback via a 360 review, or you can simply ask friends or colleagues to share their thoughts about you. Their feedback will help you to better understand yourself. Ask for honesty, let them know that you value their input, and use that information for your personal growth.

You can remove "the mud." But what's the point of self-reflection and feedback if you keep adding more sludge? How can you keep from reverting to old habits?

We want to be more like Giuseppe, with raw, uninhibited, and sincere vulnerability. How are you going to show up after that first reaction of Retreat, Fight, or Cope?

The next three points will give you more to ponder and apply.

1. Your Presence

Each of us, at any moment, is sending off various cues about how we see the world, whether we are ready to work, play, laugh, cry, fight, or move forward. If you want to attract people, it makes a difference whether you show enthusiasm, smile, and open your eyes wide in a welcoming way.

Are your voice and tone expressing openness? How many times have you called someone and just by the way they answered the phone, you were already turned off? How many times has the opposite happened? Your tone makes a world of difference, and you can feel both in your gut.

Before you focus all your energies on what you want to say or do, spend more time understanding how you are and the way you will deliver your message. I had to start paying careful attention to how I was showing up because my facial expressions wouldn't let me hide my emotions. Many of us are this way. My friends, people close to me, and particularly my daughter, were quick to tell me when they felt something bothered me, when I seemed off, or when I wasn't in the happiest of moods. I wear my emotions, as Shakespeare put it, "on my sleeve."

Before I was made aware of it, I was often caught having "Resting Bitch Face," which for me was more like "Resting Disgruntled Face." This face appeared with too much frequency when I was deep in my thoughts, worried, or stressed about work. I would show up rigid and intense (and there are deep worry lines on my forehead to show for it). People were affected by how I looked and carried myself even before I uttered the first word. I didn't realize that my expressions and general composure spoke volumes.

2. Your Voice

We often don't pay enough attention to our most powerful communication tool: our voice. Chris Voss, an FBI hostage negotiator, in his book *Never Split the Difference*, writes about three tones available to negotiators: 1) the late-night FM DJ voice, 2) the positive/playful voice, and 3) the direct or assertive voice.

He doesn't recommend using the assertive voice, except in very rare circumstances. It signals dominance to your counterpart, who will either aggressively, or passive-aggressively, push back against such communication. Instead, Voss recommends using the positive/playful voice, as it conveys an easygoing, good-natured person with a light, encouraging attitude.

Relax and smile while you're talking. Even if people don't see you, your jovial tone has an impact that the other person will pick up.

Remember the time I was crossing the border from Tibet to Nepal? My tone of voice and gesturing were the only communication tools I had, and they worked cross-culturally. How you use your voice will help you to create rapport more quickly and make or break your relationships.

3. Mirroring

Another method that will help you enhance rapport may be a little less familiar. Mirroring is the subconscious replication of another person's nonverbal signals. We often naturally do this in everyday interactions, and it usually goes unnoticed by both parties (the person mirroring and the one being mirrored). It could be as simple as a smile. Smiling people tend to inspire others to smile, and vice versa.

Emulating often begins in infancy. Babies mimic individuals around them and establish rapport with specific body movements and gestures. That connection creates a sense of empathy and an understanding of others' emotions. Likewise, mirroring can help adults establish rapport with each other, as similarities with our nonverbal gestures allow individuals to feel more connected.

Now, what's interesting is how you can mirror people by focusing on words only. You might mirror someone unconsciously with tone of voice, accent, slang, formal, or informal language.

Think of times when you have felt completely out of place while conversing with people who were speaking street language or a different language entirely. On the other hand, there may have been times when familiarity and connection were created immediately because of similarities in language, vocabulary, or idioms.

The words you communicate with have great importance. As Chris Voss wrote, "Of all the FBI's hostage negotiation skill set, mirroring, like repeating the last three words of what someone just said, is the closest one gets to a Jedi mind trick. Simple and yet very effective."

Voss also references a study by psychologist Richard Wiseman, who set up two scenarios with waiters in a restaurant. One group of waiters lavished praise and encouragement on their customers and their meal choices (e.g., "Great choice!" and "That's my favorite!"). The second group simply mirrored their customers by repeating their orders back to them. The tips received by the second group were 70 percent higher than those who used flattery and positive reinforcement.

All right, how are you doing so far? A lot comes into play in communication, right? It might make you think, "Boy, this stuff is complex. I should stop communicating altogether and just live alone in a cave." Well, it's not that dire or difficult, and you will incorporate most of these tools unconsciously once you've become mindful of them.

If I were to look at a thousand lines of code, mathematical deductions, or complex construction blueprints, I'd feel overwhelmed. And yet, when we break things down, we see how the various "ingredients" simply build upon each other. It's the same with communication. Just as lines of code, one by one, create an application, so do we build our emotional intelligence with small, incremental changes in our communication style.

As you can see, many facets of communication need to be adapted to the specific setting, the person you communicate with, and your current attitudes, perceptions, and emotions. So how do you best prepare for that? You must take the time to set an intention about how you want to be in that moment. If you do this and you adjust accordingly, you'll be able to lead conversations to more positive outcomes and foster a more positive professional image.

By the way, I checked back with Giuseppe's mother a few months later and found out that he was taking tennis lessons. Of course, being young, he has all the time in the world to do so. But even though we may have less flexibility in our schedules, we can still reach our goals with a similar ease and simplicity.

I'm also grateful for that experience with Giuseppe because it reminded me of how much more fun life is without insecurities hampering our endeavors. It encouraged me to become more self-aware and to pay attention to my emotions, self-doubts, and gremlin-limiting beliefs. Without them, life is just a lot more fun.

Questions:

- How different would your life be if you could be as free as Giuseppe?
- What would happen if you paid more attention to your triggers? What are those triggers, and how can you better respond to them?
- What is your default operating mode—Retreat, Fight, or Cope—and what leads you there? What would it be like if you could step out of these negative modes?
- What does your "discomfort detector" reveal to you?
- What about your tone of voice, attitude, and facial expressions? Do you understand how to project your true self to others?
- Do you, like me, have a "Resting Disgruntled Face"?

Chapter 12

They Are Fine; They Can Take It

Don't assume your partner wants to be led

In the film *The Godfather*, the four Corleone brothers meet right after their father, Vito Corleone (played by Marlon Brando), is shot. They debate how to retaliate against Virgil "The Turk" Sollozzo, who ordered the hit. There is a moment when Michael Corleone (Al Pacino), the youngest brother and the only one not involved in the family's mafia business, offers to be the one to avenge their father and shoot Virgil. His brothers want him to understand that retaliation is not personal, it's just business. They tell him this has nothing to do with emotions, family, or the need for justice. Rather, it's about protecting their business and sending a message to "the community."

Over the course of my career, I've worked with many managers who reminded me a bit of these brothers. Their attitude was, of course, nothing like the Corleones', and so far I have not seen or coached anyone who would walk around the conference room with a baseball bat or leave a horse's head in a rival's bed. However, I've often worked with the type of leader who tends to push and control and consider their actions merely "business." Often, these leaders haven't been aware of their attitude and have had to be nudged into coaching because—as brilliant as they are—the damage they have caused to relationships and peers has started to affect their work and projects.

Such clients were regularly accused of such things as not trusting the team; not sharing enough; intimidating, not delegating; not asking for input; using a commanding/telling voice; not asking for help; and masking their vulnerabilities. Many of these impressions are created when someone tries to stay in control by keeping others at a distance. For leaders who operate in this mode, the focus is on personal interest rather than team growth.

For example, let's take Daniel. He's a brilliant director of engineering working for a successful high-tech company in Silicon Valley. His contributions to the team are unquestioned. He is highly regarded and is considered a strong and innovative voice in his organization. Because of these qualities, his peers and reports look up to him, but, as I learned, they also feel intimidated by him. When I heard this, I got curious. I wanted to know more about his interactions and communication style. What in his attitude was causing his coworkers' responses?

I asked Daniel how he addressed people on his team. He told me he was direct and to the point. He was aware that, when giving his team feedback, he tended to use strong language and could be a bit brusque at times. However, he assured me, "Most people who work with me are OK with that type of communication. They can take it."

"They can take it?" I said. "What makes you think that?"

He shrugged, looking away. "I don't know," he said. "People on my team usually acknowledge what I tell them and then go back to work. They don't seem flustered by how or what I share. I know there are sometimes cultural differences, but my team knows my style, and they are fine with it."

"Interesting," I said. "Has anyone ever mentioned anything to you about this?"

"No, my team and I have known each other for a while. We've gone out for drinks, some of them have come over to my house for dinner. We're quite open with each other. If they didn't like how I talked to them, I'm sure they'd say something to me."

"I'm glad you have such a great rapport with them," I said. "But I wonder about your assumption that they are not bothered by the type of direct language you use."

That conversation happened early in our coaching engagement, in what I call the "discovery phase." A few weeks later, I administered a 360-feedback assessment for

Daniel, and I interviewed the participants.

The responses I received from Daniel's colleagues stood in stark contrast to Daniel's beliefs about their being able to "take it." Virtually everybody in his team asked for changes to how he interacted with them. Among their grievances were that he jumped too much into advising them and resolved issues rather than building their skills; didn't trust the team's capabilities to resolve matters on their own; wasn't open and authentic enough; didn't ask for help or share his vulnerabilities; and made his peers or reports feel intimidated to the point of their not asking for his help because they felt judged.

Most of them wanted him to share more about his plans and use more collaborative and empowering language in their interactions. They wanted him to let people fail if it helped them grow, then mentor/coach them; to delegate more, and be less in the details; to ask the team what they thought about projects and get them involved in the decisions; and to understand people's personalities and adjust the way he managed them.

Mind you, Daniel was open to feedback; he wanted to grow and was ready to be challenged. But he quickly came to a conclusion that I have heard many times from other executives. "You know, Roberto," he told me, "these people are professionals with degrees and experience in this work. They should have the knowledge to do their job, that's what we pay them for. Why do we have to be tiptoeing around when they make a mistake or don't do a good job?"

Whenever I hear that kind of sentiment, it's almost always delivered with a hint of contempt. His point was obvious: *I'm not here to babysit; I'm here to deliver results. We have timelines, and customers are expecting our products. I don't have time to explain things they should already know.*

If you think that kind of response is uncommon, think again. I hear it all the time. You might think you don't act that way; there too, think again. We all do, including me. I've been there many times, causing resentment and discord. In hindsight, I wish someone had stuck a sock in my mouth. I've all too often had a bully's condescending Corleone attitude.

All right, so what to do here?

One of my online coaching sessions with Daniel proved to be a lucky break. In the middle of the session, his nine-year-old son walked into his office. The boy waved his little hand at the camera of his father's computer; I waved back and smiled. Daniel muted his microphone and pointed his forefinger up, signaling that he'd need a minute with his son. I nodded and watched the interaction that followed.

Daniel turned and faced his son at eye level. The child said something to Daniel, who smiled and put a hand on his shoulder. They exchanged a few words. I could tell his son was asking a question. Daniel responded, and then I saw the boy look up and away. It looked like he was reflecting on a question. He then responded. Daniel nodded and his son smiled. They hugged, and then the boy left the room.

Daniel turned to me and unmuted his microphone. "He had questions about his homework," he said.

"And it looks like he got a satisfactory answer," I replied, smiling. Then we continued with our coaching session.

These kinds of interludes often happen when sessions are later in the day, and they frequently occurred during the pandemic. The scene is always the same: children come in, my client is surprised and turns to them, the one-minute finger goes up, and they mute their microphone. Now, Daniel's son coming into the room on that particular day, however, was the best thing that could have happened. Here's why: After his son left, I said, "Daniel, I couldn't hear you, but it looked like you had a good interaction with your son there. You were looking him straight in the eye. You said something, and then he felt satisfied and left. If I may ask, could you tell me what type of language you are using with your children, in general?"

He wasn't sure where I was going with that. He asked, "Do you mean how do I talk to my kids?"

"Yes. If you had to put this in work terms, how would you describe your 'parenting leadership'?"

He thought about it for a moment, then said something like, "Hmm, interesting question. I'd say that I would want my children to feel cared for and supported but also to be strong and self-sufficient. I mean, I don't want to have to deal with my kids and support them for the rest of my life."

"Ah, of course," I said. "I'm a parent myself, and we want our children to get to a point where they can walk out into the world and be able to manage all sorts of challenges and survive—strong, healthy, and fulfilled."

Then I added, "We want that so that our kids can be independent, and, let's not hide it, we want to get to a point where we can relax, enjoy our happy-hour drinks, and not have to worry about our grown children being out there on their own, right?"

"Yes, absolutely!" he said.

"And what's interesting is that we do this for our kids, but we don't do it at work."

Daniel, like most people, said, "Well, it's not the same, my team is paid for their work."

His objection went to the heart of the problem.

Yes, his team members are paid for their work, but they are not just employees. We forget that people are people, no matter their age, title, degrees, or role they hold in the workplace.

I shared that with him, and then said, "Daniel, underneath all those titles and roles, there is a human being who wants to be addressed the way you were addressing your son earlier. Your son wanted to be seen, as do your reports."

This is important.

Let me repeat it: people are people.

Stop looking at the outer layers and the work uniform; consider instead what's underneath. Look at people in your workforce as human beings who want to know that they matter, that their ideas matter, that you care for them, and that you will support them in becoming more self-sufficient and confident.

If you can view and treat your coworkers that way, not only will that empower them, it will also allow you to better focus on other more critical objectives.

So how do we do this? Given the responses to Daniel's 360 feedback, and given his perception of his coworkers and his need for control, there were two main points that needed to be addressed:

1. How our unhealthy need for control can profoundly affect us and the people we work and interact with; and

2. How we need to pay attention to our perceptions of other people, particularly to how we think our team or peers perceive us.

Let's take a closer look at what causes our need for control and what shapes our perceptions, so we can better understand how to work with them.

Control Is a Trap That Stems from a Place of Fear and Scarcity

Control comes from the ego, and its main function is to tie you to your present self. It is a function of self-preservation and of maintaining the status quo and will therefore not let you extend yourself in your growth.

Most people don't even realize how controlling they are. They might seem happy in control because they achieve business results, save the company money, or keep stakeholders satisfied. So when leaders are blamed for being control freaks, they think, "Hey, I'm only doing my job and getting work done. Someone has to push, or we would miss deadlines and fall behind."

For a short time, that sort of power may work, but no one likes to be controlled or ordered around in the long term. When someone is controlled for too long, that person will want to get out of that constraining environment and instead work in a place where their contribution is valued and they can feel more independent.

When you control others, you don't influence or inspire them; instead, you restrict and dampen their creativity, innovation, and growth. Moreover, being in a position of control uses an enormous amount of energy that goes into protecting our fragile egos and maintaining the facade.

Psychological research has underscored how much time and energy is wasted on self-protection; in fact, it is considered a leading cause of waste of an organization's resources. Bob Kegan and Lisa Lahey explain that the proclivity for control comes from the natural tendency people have for "preserving their reputations, putting their best selves forward, and hiding their inadequacies from others and themselves."[9]

Jennifer Garvey Berger, in *Unlocking Leadership Mindtraps*, writes, "When we try to defend our egos rather than grow and change, we end up perfectly designed for a world that happened already, instead of growing better able to handle the world that is coming next."[10]

Reading through the 360-assessment report and seeing what others had written about him was hard for Daniel. I felt his pain. The experience was shattering his "they can take it" beliefs, which meant that he would have to rethink how he viewed others.

---

[9]https://hbr.org/2014/04/making-business-personal

[10]Berger, G. J. *Unlocking Leadership Mindtraps: How to Thrive in Complexity,* 1st ed. (Stanford Briefs, 2019), 20.

There was work to do, and the work that needed to happen was a direct challenge to his Corleone mindset ("it's not personal, it's only business"). He would need to adapt his language and change his energy to one that was directed toward support and care for his team. He would need to explore what responsibilities he felt comfortable sharing with others, with vulnerability, to influence them and achieve the results collaboratively.

He needed to address his colleagues not with a "they can take it" attitude but with a "how can I help you?" mindset. It wouldn't be easy for Daniel. But I knew that simply asking how he could help would have the power to shift the way he was thinking and expand his perspective. And I knew it would also change the way he was perceiving others and how others were perceiving him.

Perceptions Matter

Daniel and I discussed what it is that makes us human as well as how our cultural differences shape us. He's from Eastern Europe and I'm an Italian who grew up in Switzerland; both of us have worked extensively with companies in the United States.

We agreed that how we interact was determined by the "layering" of our cultural and personal upbringing—that the mix of those factors is what makes us who we are, shaping the ways we respond to people.

Our "layers" are established by our beliefs, thoughts, emotions, upbringing, and experiences, among other influences. Some of these layers negatively affect us, while other layers have a positive effect, elevate the way we respond, and give us access to more positive interaction and outcomes.

Our level of consciousness determines how we respond to each situation. In short, it's as if all the layers that we have accumulated over time are now affecting the way we view the world. Look at it this way: if you are wearing purple glasses, everything will appear purple to you. Wear another color, and everything will look that color. Your background and current perceptions determine your reality. So, in Daniel's case, the glasses he was wearing determined how he perceived others and how he thought they would receive his comments. His glasses are saying that people "can take it" because:

1. He might believe that *he* can take it, so why not also his team?
2. His colleagues don't mind because they don't say anything back.
3. No one quit; they still work there and hang out with him for drinks.

Therefore, they must like him.

Yes, all three points are plausible, but that's only from Daniel's perspective, through his colored glasses. What others experience might be completely different. And as Daniel realized from the feedback, people working with him indeed viewed his work style quite differently.

The color of his team's glasses was different. Their perceptions were affected by layers of hurtful and demeaning incidents, what we might call microaggressions. The slow buildup of sharp little stabs, over time, had started to affect how people in the team saw themselves, how they interacted with their peers, and how they engaged with their work. You've probably heard it said many times that "people don't leave their jobs, they leave their managers."

Make It Personal

Nobody likes working with someone who has a *Godfatherly* attitude of "not making things personal." Quite the opposite, to build collaboration and inspire your workforce, you *must* make things personal.

Your team wants to look up to you and know that you'll be there to support them. They will deliver on your objectives and give their very best as long as you make them part of the plan and help them understand how much you appreciate their efforts, creativity, and dedication. In short, you need to get your ego out of the way and be there when needed. No one wants to steal your algorithms; rather, they want to see how you've resolved them so they can learn from you and perhaps help you down the line.

After several months of our working together, Daniel started to see a shift around him as he began to be less involved in the team meetings and only interjected when necessary. He began delegating responsibilities to peers and people who had already demonstrated their abilities. He also started to share with them his overall plans and clarify his expectations so they could see the role they played in the whole project.

Even Daniel's supervisor commended him for his newly found composure in addressing his team and empowering it. Slowly, Daniel allowed himself to become more transparent about sharing his concerns, stating his worries about projects, and asking for the team's input. This transparency and vulnerability also helped him strengthen relationships.

In the past, people had deferred responsibilities to him. Now they knew that he would bounce the questions and concerns back at them and that he would ask them to find their own solutions. As a result, they refrained from asking him in the first place. And the more they did so, the more they became empowered, confident, and efficient.

Questions:

- What is your overall mode of operating? Are you holding back information?
- Are you aware of your biases in how you address people?
- Do you have a "they can take it" mindset when you talk to your coworkers?
- Have you ever approached things along the lines of "this is just business, nothing personal"?

Chapter 13

Stop Telling Them What to Do—Coach Them Instead

Ask, ask, and then ask your dance partner again

In our third coaching session, I asked Brian, a senior project manager in a large high-tech company, "Can you think of a manager or leader you've worked with that you look up to and admire?"

He didn't hesitate. "Oh, for me, it's definitely my boss, Scott."

"Can you tell me about him?"

"You know," he said, "what's interesting about Scott is that when I meet with him, I always have to prepare answers because he asks me a lot of questions."

"Ha, interesting. And what do you think about that?" I asked.

"I'm not sure how to say this," he said, "but it makes me feel like he wants to know about my thoughts and ideas. And that makes me feel good because he cares to know how I work and doesn't just tell me what to do. It makes me believe he trusts my work."

He added, "I kind of feel good about myself when I'm done talking with him."

"That's wonderful," I said. "Do you know what Scott is doing? Your boss is using a coaching mindset."

A coaching mindset is very important for life in general but particularly for work. Research has shown that the ability to effectively coach is key to enabling innovation, creativity, resilience, trust, and accelerated team growth. No wonder it's directly linked to improved business performance and increased revenues.

As a leader, your main responsibility is not only business development but most importantly, human development—which includes both your own evolution as well as the growth of the people you lead. With a coaching mindset, you can step out of being the sole solution provider.

The constant barrage of business and management problems can easily render your workload untenable and cause you to become a bottleneck. By asking questions and listening well, you can empower your team to bring ideas, grow their skills, and ease your workload.

Brian's manager recognized the potential in Brian and knew how to address him in a way that leveraged his knowledge and gave him the confidence to tackle new challenges. The manager believed Brian was fully capable of finding solutions and reinforced that belief in him. Now, that's what competent leaders do, and the result is an empowered individual who not only feels confident in the work he does but is also autonomous and excited to work with his boss.

So, what did Brian's boss do exactly? What does it look like to use a coaching mindset? And why don't we use the coaching mindset more? Let's start by looking at what the coaching mindset is. It includes the following essential skills, in no particular order:

1. **Seeing Potential**

2. **Being Curious**

3. **Active Listening**

4. **Knowing About Yourself and Staying in Control and Neutral**

5. **Honoring Choices**

6. **Knowing How to Ask Questions**

7. **Transferring Ownership**

Let's take a closer look at these seven skills.

Seeing Potential

It's essential to go into a conversation with the right mindset, i.e., considering the conversation partner competent. I've talked at length in previous chapters about adopting the right mindset before you even start your conversations. Well, here, it's even more critical.

If you initiate a dialogue with the intention of helping someone but don't really believe that person has the ability to do it, guess what? You probably will be using all the wrong words.

They'll sense your attitude a mile away, even before you attempt to help them. Assuming "what you see is what you get" is never helpful. But if you believe there is more to a person than meets the eye, you will naturally try to bring that to the table.

Being Curious

I can scarcely express how important this is: curiosity is at the base of everything. It's not enough to consider curiosity in light of what we desire to know more of; we need to also understand what it is that blocks our curiosity and makes us rigid (something I was guilty of far too often in my early days).

When rigid and self-righteous, we'll often disregard others' points of view, and that in turn prevents us from seeing alternative outcomes. Rigidity locks us in our old habits, we don't really listen anymore, and we effectively shut down others' ideas. We can get so trapped in our rightfulness that we discard anything that might prove us wrong. That's the end of curiosity, right there.

We all want to be right, that is understandable, but wanting to be right stifles our sense of wonder. In her book *Unlocking Leadership Mindtraps*, Jennifer Garvey Berger writes that when people are exposed to new ideas and projects, their response falls into one of three types: Defensive and Confident, Annoyed and Offended, or Open and Curious. Rarely does anyone embrace the third option, Open and Curious, and that's due to our sense of righteousness.

However, when we ask ourselves, "Hmm, how might I be wrong, or what might I be missing?" we allow ourselves to be more flexible and curious, and that in turn will help others overcome their own rigidity.

Active Listening

My friend Laura just told me about visiting her friend Monica, who was feeling low and, having recently experienced challenging events in her life, borderline depressed. After just a few hours together, Monica told Laura that she felt much better. "So," I asked Laura, "what did you do to make her feel better?"

"Not much," answered Laura. "I just asked how she was doing and then I listened to her. I didn't say anything really, other than nodding and acknowledging her pain. Monica talked, cried, talked some more and cried again, and after a few hours she said, 'You know, I feel better. It's lighter now. I wish it could be like this all the time.'"

Then Laura told me, "You know, all she wanted was to be heard and recognized for the pain she was experiencing. I don't think she needed any advice at this point."

And that is precisely what listening is all about. Stand back, let it flow, and don't think about answers. Just let the other person breathe out their pain, their worries, their dreams and visions. Let them share and liberate themselves. If they need more, they'll ask you. If you feel they are stuck, you can probe them with a question. Listening means just that: making an effort to be actively focused on the other person.

Knowing About Yourself and Staying in Control and Neutral

Being in the coaching mindset means staying centered, controlling your ego, and not letting yourself fall into judgmental and opinionated modes. In a coaching conversation, you want to remain neutral and self-aware. After all, it's not about you but about what the other person is experiencing. To stay fully open, you must let go of your own biases and opinions.

Make it your intention to see the other person as fully capable of finding a solution, even if that solution is not what you would have chosen. If needed, help them by building from where they stand, and if you have something of benefit to offer, it's OK to just plant a seed, asking, "What do you think of the 'seed'?" and "How does this 'seed' resonate with you?" This way, you allow them to make the idea their own.

Honoring Choices

When people feel their ideas matter, they are more creative and innovative in their work. Free to be themselves, they will tap into their inner ingenuity to approach any obstacles they face. When we witness this happening, it is essential that we honor their choices so they can bring their ideas to fruition.

To foster this freedom and creativity, we need to let go of control and allow ourselves to be surprised. Sure, that's easier said than done, but just imagine a world in which there were no room for experimentation, growth, and creativity.

Knowing How to Ask Questions

The power of coaching relies on the coach's ability to ask cogent, important questions. After you listen with curiosity and focus to the person you want to coach, you will need to know when and how to ask questions that foster reflection, inner clarity, and empowerment. As a coach, you are not an advisor but a facilitator of growth.

The coaching mindset is about guiding wisdom and leadership in its truest and noblest sense. Twenty-five hundred years ago, the *Tao Te Ching* recognized the hallmarks of a great master. Verse 17 reads:

"When the Master governs, the people
are hardly aware that he exists.
Next best is a leader who is loved.
Next, one who is feared.
The worst is one who is despised.
If you don't trust the people,
you make them untrustworthy.
The Master doesn't talk, he acts.
When his work is done,
the people say, "Amazing:
we did it, all by ourselves!"

Transferring Ownership

Anybody who has ever built up another person with the intent of ultimately making this person free and independent, any teacher, parent, or true leader, understands the importance of "transferring ownership."

I have a daughter in her early twenties who is in her last year of college and becoming fully independent. Soon she'll go out into the world, look for a job, get an apartment, and file taxes on her own (some of which she is already doing).

While she is growing more and more self-reliant, I'm sitting here in my backyard, typing away, and concentrating on this book. At night, I am able to sleep well, I do not worry about her. If we have parented well, we have raised our children to become fully autonomous. We have challenged them, educated them, and fostered their independence so that one day, when we are no longer around, they will thrive on their own, competently and confidently.

That's what I mean by "transferring ownership." In your conversations, you are going to do everything that's needed to make sure your clients, colleagues, or reports are ready to walk solo, confident, and autonomous. You certainly don't want them to become what Italians call a *mammone* (mama's boy), who is still living with his parents in his forties.

Before moving into the practical application of these concepts, let's take a moment to consider the most common stumbling block coaches and teachers run into: the propensity to give advice.

I understand how well-intended it is to give advice, how naturally it comes to us, and how often the recipient really appreciates the generosity; in the best-case scenario, people on both sides of advice will benefit. Moreover, when given "softly," advice can provide orientation and even inspiration.

Advice takes no time, gets things moving, makes you feel good and your team grateful. So, why on earth would it be considered a stumbling block?

The reason is simple, commonsensical, and proven by neuroscience. Advice discourages the receiver from exercising self-leadership. It robs people of their innate ability to be creative and find their own solution. And it erodes self-accountability.

Brain research has shown that our minds tend to go into passive mode when we receive advice. I'm sure you've seen people tune out during a presentation, even though they continue to listen. A similar process happens when we are getting advice. Rather than actively engaging in the search for solutions, our brain just softly hums along; we are, in essence, checking out.

Michael Bungay Stanier, author of *The Advice Trap*, discusses the "three advice monsters": Tell It, Save the World, and Control It.

The Tell It persona enjoys being seen as intelligent; his ego gets a boost from providing solutions. The Save the World persona likes the idea of rescuing others, as he or she thinks it will make him a hero. The Control It persona needs to be dominant and gets frustrated when things don't go their way.

To understand why we fall so easily into one of these categories, we have to understand why this tendency is so ingrained in us.

I grew up in the 1970s, and my parents were the kind who told my two siblings and me what to do; either we did it or we'd "get it." There was no positive reinforcement. We knew we did a good job when we didn't get yelled at or smacked in the back of the head. It was never abusive, just a "realignment," so to speak, that included loud words and stern faces.

It was efficient in the short term because we got stuff done, and it was easy for my parents to keep their ducks in a row. If we messed up, my parents would put us back on task and have us practice it repeatedly until we got it right. And this strategy wasn't just for small household tasks; construction work, house painting, car maintenance, and house chores were also part of our job description.

My parents would say, *"Il lavoro si fa con amore,"* which means "Work is done with love." Well, the love in our family was never missing; however, I can't say we loved that highly "pedagogic" parenting style, nor all the work we had to do. It engrained in me a rigidity and a whole slew of behavioral patterns that I had to work hard to unlearn later in life.

Not long ago, a coaching client asked me how to tell people what to do without being too direct. I asked him why he wanted to know that, and his reply was quite clear: "Well, I hate it when people tell *me* what to do."

"And why is that?" I asked.

"Because I know how to do my work, and if I don't, I'll figure it out. And if I need support, I'll ask. But *I* want to decide when to reach out."

His was a typical answer. When people feel that their

choices are restricted by others telling them what to do, they will resist, regardless of whether the feedback was helpful. They tend to rebel or even do the opposite. Psychologists call this phenomenon "psychological reactance."[11] It's our brain's response to a threat to our freedom (being told what and how to do something). People will defend their independence by acting in "direct restoration" of their autonomy. For example, when asked to put the seat belt on before leaving the driveway, some of us might not do so right away because we want to keep our decision autonomy (yes, that would be me!).

In summary, the advice-giving management style comes at a high cost:

- You'll be spending far too much time solving other people's issues.
- You'll be holding them back from using their full potential, affecting teams' results.
- They will be dependent on you and will lack confidence.
- You will be overwhelmed and exhausted, and it will affect the way you react to people.

And there are consequences for the people you advise:
- They will be stunted in their growth.
- They will become dependent.
- They will question their every move, wondering what the advice-dispenser will think. (If this is you: Bravo, you've now become a bottleneck!)

---

[11]Christina Steindl, Eva Jonas, Sandra Sittenthaler, Eva Traut-Mattausch, and Jeff Greenberg, "Understanding Psychological Reactance" (*Zeitschrift fur Psychologie*, 2015).

- They will be less engaged and will lose interest in their work very fast.

- They'll be thinking about happy hour while you're still talking their ears off.

OK, now that I've laid out the main reasons why not to give advice, take a moment to consider your own motivations and actions:

1. What drives you to answer questions and advise people?

2. What if you didn't answer them? What could happen that might be positive?

3. In what circumstances do you tend to give advice? When do you not?

4. In what situations do you think you could start shifting from advice-giver to one who empowers others?

Let's look at what we can do instead.

We can use a **coaching framework** that's easy to remember and apply. This framework provides a logical step-by-step coaching structure that can be applied in either a ten-minute conversation or a one-hour meeting. Before we get into this framework, however, let's take a separate look at a key element of any successful coaching session: the power of meaningful questions.

Ask Meaningful Questions

Asking meaningful questions is a skill that goes to the heart of living and learning. Much of the success in our career and our personal life depends on how and what questions we ask, and what decisions we make based on what we learn.

The best teachers and leaders will inspire reflection by asking questions. They can engage and teach a team how to be curious about themselves and their beliefs. Meaningful and creative questions will spur critical thinking, and critical thinking is far more powerful than spoon-fed answers. It can inspire curiosity and a deep understanding of personal barriers and ways of overcoming them.

To ask powerful questions, you need to involve all your faculties, your whole self, really, including logic and gut feelings. Have you ever had someone tell you about a challenge or a goal, and halfway through the conversation, your gut tells you that something isn't quite right, that something is amiss here? If you are listening well, your curiosity will light up and you will gently probe for more information.

Visualize that person as an iceberg. The tip of the iceberg represents his outer world, the part that is seen and manifest, the part he wants you to know about him. Asking thought-provoking questions and listening deeply, however, you can learn more about the "hidden" part of the iceberg— his underlying attitude and behavior, his values, beliefs, biases, fears, hopes, emotions, and judgments. Just by being curious and attentive (while remaining neutral), you will recognize whether somebody is sharing something from the tip of the iceberg or from their submerged inner world.

I once worked with a client, Natalie, who started every session by pointing at external reasons for not getting what she wanted at work. She'd say, "The team is not helping me find solutions" instead of "I struggle to find solutions," or "My colleagues are not supporting me in my work" instead of "I'm having a hard time resolving this on my own."

Do you hear the difference? In expecting external changes, Natalie failed to recognize that she needed to take a look within herself, below the surface, to find the reasons for her frustration. Figuring this out required internal exploration, not external blaming. I knew that she would eventually need the courage to ask for help, but that in turn meant that she had to reveal her vulnerability, and she was not quite ready for that.

Here is how to approach a conversation similar to the one I had with Natalie, using an inward-focused coaching framework:

- Ask open-ended questions as much as you can. Yes/no questions limit answers, while open-ended questions help clients elaborate on their thoughts. For example, ask:
  - How are you feeling today? (vs. Are you feeling better today?)
  - What is happening with the project? (vs. Have you finished the project?)
  - How can I support you? (vs. Do you need support?)

- Usually, if you start a question with "When," "What," "Who," or "How," you are going to ask an open-ended question. However, be careful with the "Why" questions and your tone of voice when asking them, to avoid sounding judgmental.

- Your intent to support the person rather than just gather information from them will change your tone of voice, your presence, and how they perceive you. When, for example, you meet with somebody you consider smart and capable, your attitude will be far more positive than if you think the person dull and incapable. Our attitude changes the way we show up energetically.

- Finally, one essential point I always share with participants who want to learn about the coaching mindset is that they shouldn't get stuck in trying to find the right question to ask. Instead of wondering what to ask next, think about what you want to know next. If you listen well and follow your curiosity, it'll help you know what questions to ask. I'll show you a series of questions that can help you later in this chapter, but even with the list, you'll always have to follow your curiosity and what you sense first.

So, to support Natalie in exploring what was happening below the surface, I asked her, "What makes you think your colleagues are not supporting you?", "What could happen if you asked for support?", and "In what areas do you feel you need support?"

These questions were meant to initiate the process of finding her own solutions. I encouraged her to explore a course change and asked about realistic steps she might take. Once she identified a few modifications to her behavior, I asked how committed she was to the change, what she could do to maintain her changes of behavior, and how she would hold herself accountable.

Meaningful questions are the foundation of a coaching mindset. In the next section, I'll provide a more detailed framework that outlines the five key elements of one-on-one conversations. They are simple and will help you establish initial goals, clarify your conversation partner's experience, and identify the challenges. With those in mind, you'll be able to help explore solutions and offer guidance in implementing them.

In the appendix, you'll find sample questions for each category as well as a coaching dialogue. While these questions are meant to be helpful (particularly in the beginning), they should not be a substitute for using your own curiosity. Ultimately, when engaging with a client, you want to always follow your gut feeling.

The Coaching Framework

The coaching framework includes five elements:

1. **Purpose**
2. **Circumstances**
3. **Acknowledgment**
4. **Opportunities**
5. **Ownership**

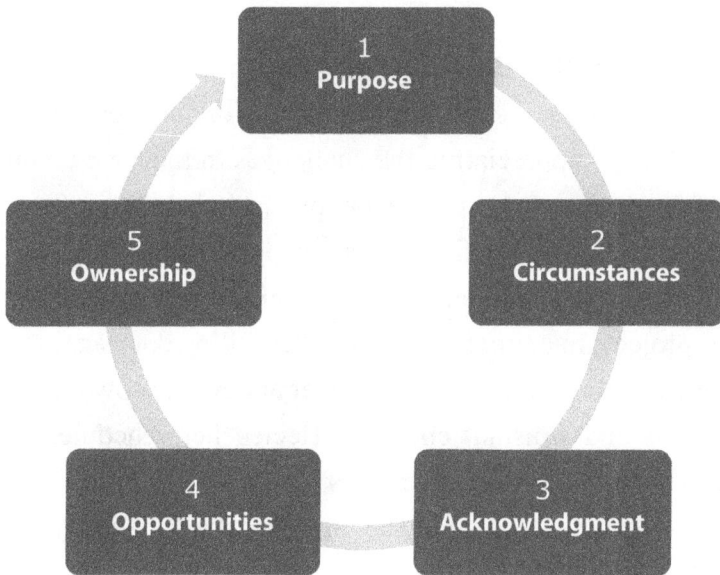

1. Defining Purpose

It is critical to define performance goals and agree on desired outcomes. To do so, you need to first know what is going on, why somebody wants to talk to you, and/or get an update on a specific project. A few sample questions you could ask are:

- What's on your mind?
- What would you like to discuss?
- What are you currently experiencing?
- What are you hoping, as a result of our conversation, to be able to do more of, do less of, or do differently? (If they are vague in their response, you can say: I heard several things; which do you want to focus on?)

The point is simply to gain a clear understanding of the discussion at hand. I'll provide more examples later.

2. Understanding the Circumstances

All too often, people try to set goals or solve problems without fully appreciating the challenges in their way. You need your clients to explain what precisely is holding them back and what difficulties they are experiencing.

For example, a client told me about her struggle to deliver projects in a timely fashion. After failing once again to meet a deadline, she expressed anger at how her coworkers' demands and constant changes affected her schedule; on the surface, these "circumstances" caused the delays.

As we got deeper into the analysis, she began to realize that the culprit wasn't so much the external challenges as it was her inability to push back on demands and say no to proposed changes; the "circumstances" was her lack of assertiveness.

Without inquiring into the deeper circumstances, we might have just accepted her first diagnosis without realizing the underlying conditions. So, it's essential to stay with the questions and gather all the information needed to overcome the barriers and implement corrective actions. A few questions to help discover what circumstances a client is facing might be:

- What is the current situation?
- What realistic barriers exist to successfully complete your goal?
- What is not working well in your life/work/team, etc.?
- What are the consequences to you/your team?
- Where does change need to happen—internally or externally?

While the person describes the circumstances, remain curious all along. If you listen, roll with what they share, and ask powerful questions, you will allow for solutions to develop.

3. Acknowledging the Situation

What does it mean to acknowledge somebody? It can be as simple as making that person feel heard and validated—even small efforts at acknowledgment can mean so much. A simple form of acknowledgment is to paraphrase or repeat the gist of somebody's circumstances: "So, what I heard you say is . . ." Making sure that you got it right will make the other person feel seen and understood.

Acknowledging somebody's circumstances is impor-tant, but it is just as important to validate the person's expe-rience of the circumstances—particularly when that person is having a hard time.

Imagine a report of yours is having difficulties with buggy software. He feels he is lacking support, and—making matters worse—a colleague just got sick, leaving him to work on the application alone. You could say something as simple as, "Hey, it must have been hard to take on all the burden yourself this past week. No wonder you are stressed, tired, and frustrated." In the first part, you acknowledge what has happened; in the second, you validate the person's emotions of stress, frustration, or tiredness.

Once he feels supported and knows that his opinions and struggles matter, he will probably exhale and visibly relax. He feels *seen.*

The simple act of acknowledgment will help him let go of the circumstances so that he can focus on the next steps.

4. Exploring Opportunities and Possibilities

At this stage, you can engage your conversation partner in what I call a "transforming dialogue." He now has his solutions and is ready to hit the road, and so you want to increase his motivation, build confidence, and inspire commitment. To get him excited about the opportunities, you may ask:

- What possible outcomes could come from changing course?
- What advantages do you foresee?
- Tell me more about how this could work for you/your team?
- What would help you? What support do you need to achieve your goals?

Transforming dialogues can help move people from facing obstacles to envisioning positive outcomes which, in turn, will give focus and purpose to their work.

At any point, be careful not to jump into advice-giving mentorship; rather, help the person reflect on his own abilities to find solutions.

Of course, you will have to adapt to your colleague or client's knowledge level. With a junior employee, you may have to offer more ideas; with senior staff, fewer directions will suffice. But no matter what level you engage on, be sure to ask a question for every seed you want to plant, see how it resonates, and find out what it takes to foster a sense of responsibility for it.

5. Modeling Ownership

Having examined the Circumstances and explored the Opportunities, your coachees will now have a good idea of how they can achieve their goal. Your final step as a coach will be to have them commit to specific actions and explore strategies to avoid relapse.

Here, you want to hear what your coachee will do next and when they'll get started. Do not summarize the conversation or remind them of next steps; if you did that, it would still be *you* who had ownership. Rather, let *them* tell you how they will move forward.

Some good coaching questions to facilitate the ownership transfer are:

- How ready are you to begin? (Here you are checking for commitment. Someone prepared will say they will start right away. Others might find excuses or barriers.)

- What precisely will you start doing more of, doing less of, or doing differently?
- How can you break it into manageable chunks? (Here we ask them to be more specific.)
- What could stop you from continuing the behavioral commitment?
- What if committing to new behaviors is more complicated than you thought?
- Who can hold you accountable and support you?
- When/how will I know about your progress?

With these questions, we are checking for grit and goal motivation. If you sense weakness, explore what could be holding them back, what's below the iceberg. Follow your gut to sense the barriers. A final question could be, "How will you celebrate?" This way, you can help them realize that there could be a great personal reward.

Don't be afraid of challenging them if you sense any doubts or weakness in how they will deliver. Continue meeting with them regularly so you can ask about progress and coach them through any hurdles.

Trust the process by focusing on what they can do more of, less of, or differently. Offer your support and encourage them to reach out to you to discuss progress. As you see them inch toward their goals, don't forget to celebrate their achievements, no matter how small.

As a coach, you have the responsibility and power to change your clients' lives. No pressure, right? But you do. Just remember that if all these questions were asked without true curiosity, your client would sense that immediately. Quality questions asked with curiosity, however, will inevitably empower them to see themselves and their capabilities.

William Miller[12] found that the amount of time spent on counseling was irrelevant compared to other, more pertinent distinctions. For one, he asserts that confrontation does not motivate change; it is simply ineffective to force people to face their struggles. Miller wondered what would happen if counselors merely helped patients figure out what it was *they* wanted rather than what their fed-up friends or colleagues wished for them.

Reframing the question, Miller discovered that the most effective way to help individuals reconnect to their overarching values and goals was to stop trying to control their thoughts and behaviors, to replace judgment with empathy, and to replace lectures with questions.

The instant we stop imposing our agenda on others, we eliminate the fight for control. The moment that fight ceases is the moment we begin to truly influence.

Miller developed a method he called "motivational interviewing." Through the use of open and nondirective questions, you can help others examine what is most important to them. Just by listening attentively, you can help a client discover on their own what they must do and what changes to make. A resistant person can be influenced only by someone willing to surrender control. If that happens,

---

[12]William Miller, PhD, "Motivational Interviewing," (psychotherapy.net, 2012).

one of the most powerful human motivations can blossom: the power of a committed heart.

The committed heart is one that is in alignment with a person's intentions, that has removed biases and is open to seeing the other person as a locus of potential and capability. Questions that come from a committed heart are one of the most powerful tools of human communication. In the appendix of this book, you will find two coaching dialogues as well as a broad range of sample questions.

Chapter 14

How to Give Them Critical Feedback— the Right Way

Feedback and recognition to improve the dance

An Italian proverb tells us that *"La lingua non ha ossa ma rompe le ossa"*—"The tongue has no bones but it breaks bones."

I know I've broken some bones and have had mine broken as well.

Giving feedback is one of the most generous acts of leadership. Great leaders and mentors have the ability to guide and motivate others without breaking bones—even if what they have to share is a hard truth. In fact, particularly when the feedback is challenging or difficult, imparting it the right way makes all the difference. You can become the person remembered as a life-changing figure or as the bone breaker.

Lisa, a program trainer in my team back when I was an instructional designer, was initially great at delivering the courses we developed. After a few months, however, gaps started to appear, her performance declined, and customers complained. We needed to address the issues.

I was not her manager, but since I was in charge of the programs she delivered, our boss asked me to give her performance feedback. Why me? I thought. Couldn't my boss tell her? I delayed the conversation for a while, but after a few weeks, I finally scheduled the dreaded meeting. I set an intention to be very clear about the issues and the need for improvement.

We met by video, online. In the beginning, she was her bubbly self, and we chitchatted about what was happening in our lives. Then I shifted the conversation to address her low evaluation scores. As soon as I did that, I saw her shrink back. Her face showing apprehension, she said, "All right. What's going on?"

"Lisa," I began, "in the past few programs I observed, I noticed that you missed several key points and your delivery was below standard. The participants were lost and had to interrupt you with questions. It showed you were not prepared, and as a result your class couldn't follow."

Lisa didn't say a word.

"I also looked at the evaluations," I continued. "Participants complained, and the scores were really low. You know," I added with scorn on my face, "that also affects my reputation and the image of our training department."

I stopped talking and sat back in my chair. Lisa was visibly upset. Her arms were now crossed, and she looked straight at me without saying a word. After a while, she broke the silence. "You know, I also saw the evaluation results, and I knew that I messed up. I've struggled with this program for a while, but you wouldn't know that because we never really had a chance to talk about it. You gave me the facilitator's guide only a week before the training started, and then left me with it." Then she added, "Could we talk about this some other time? I think I'm way too irritated now to get anything positive out of this conversation."

"Of course," I said. "Let's talk some other time."

We closed the virtual call, and I walked out of the conference room feeling horrible. I liked Lisa and had not wanted to hurt her feelings. I knew I had failed at giving her feedback. She needed to say what she said, and I sorely needed to hear it. It took a few years, however, before I understood how wrong I truly had been.

Providing feedback is challenging. People are afraid to give it and are often uncomfortable receiving it. Feedback is something we want to outsource. After all, who wants to negatively affect a relationship or cause bad feelings by having to tell someone their work needs . . . well, *work*?

It's no wonder that brain research has shown that people respond to the word *feedback* the same way they do to physical threats. Richard Farson, founder of the Western

Behavioral Sciences Institute, described in 1963's *Praise Reappraised* how the act of giving feedback, whether positive or negative, implies superiority. It can be interpreted in a way that says that if I'm allowing you to give me feedback on something that I did well on or messed up, I accept your higher status over me on that subject. It means that I am a lesser person than you and I have to recognize that you have more abilities than me.

There are, however, different ways of giving feedback that don't make the receiver want to shrivel up and die. The key here is to offer support, be empathetic, choose your words carefully, and use a tone that makes the receiver feel valued for what they do and who they are.

Giving Constructive Feedback

Let's start with how you can prepare for your discussion.

Before you even earn the right to give feedback, you must **check your intentions.** I have said this before: the content of what you have to say and its delivery method is secondary to your intentions and mindset. Always!

You must ask yourself: what is my purpose? In the case of Lisa, my intention was not to help and support her. I was, in fact, covering my back, making sure that my reputation wouldn't suffer. I expressed superiority by criticizing her work, so I didn't have to take any responsibility for the low evaluations. I pointed my finger at her and completely neglected to recognize the role I had played.

The first important lesson here is to never make it about yourself; you need to get your ego out of the way and be in service to the other. To make my conversation with Lisa productive, I would have had to shift my thinking from how I was affected to focusing on her receiving the feedback and supporting her in correcting the issues.

If your goal is simply to admonish someone for a bad job, you may as well not say anything; otherwise, you're basically being a bully. Most of the time, the individual under scrutiny already knows they screwed up.

Punishment is not the point; in fact, it's the opposite of the point.

Neuroscience research shows that positive reinforcement is far more effective than negative feedback. Had I looked at all the positives of Lisa's training delivery and not just the negatives, I could have increased her self-efficacy while helping her focus on areas of improvement.

What's essential in these conversations is that you **create a safe space** built on trust. Building rapport doesn't happen overnight, so you'll have to be even more careful if you don't already have a strong, trusting relationship with this person. Be sensitive and inclusive, and don't say anything that could make them go on the defensive. You can start the conversation with something like, "Hey, I guess we both know why we're here today. I can't imagine what must be going through your head and what you're feeling right now. If it were me, I'd probably be feeling frustrated, stressed, angry, and disappointed. How is this resonating with you?" and then wait to hear what they share.

A small introduction like that will take only a few

seconds, but it will allow them to feel that the meeting will be a dialogue rather than a one-sided accusation. No need to use my exact words; find ones that will suit your person and put them at ease.

Once you've listened and you understand their perspective, you can move into sharing the main point of the meeting. In Lisa's case, I could have said, "Lisa, I was in your last two training sessions, and I've also heard from participants and clients about the classes. The evaluation scores were lower than we expected. There must be something I don't know, I missed, or don't understand about what happened. Can you tell me what you thought of it? Can you help me better understand, so that I can help?"

With this kind of intro, you can bring up what you heard or noticed about poor performance but also allow the client to **share their side of the story.** This step is crucial because it allows someone like Lisa to feel heard and share any challenges she experienced. As the person expresses what happened, make sure to listen well and continue to ask open-ended questions.

This is when Lisa would have shared her frustration with me about not receiving the training guide early enough and about my lack of involvement in learning the program. (And, to be honest, because I didn't provide that support, I should have done some serious time in the hot seat as well.)

Now, the next step is to move into a **constructive correction.** Here you can say, "Is it OK if I share a few points?" This is a simple way to ask for permission to add your input. Don't worry; they'll say yes and appreciate you asking and easing them into it.

Then you explain what happened. You can talk about the impact their performance had on the project, service, or people. Don't go on at great length, keep your feedback brief, and pause to ask them questions and listen. The questions could be, "What do you think about what I just shared?" or "What are your observations about what happened?" Here you start shifting into the Coaching Framework. Listen to them, acknowledge what you hear, and then move into the Opportunities section of the coaching model, before defining a corrective behavior.

Ask them to take ownership of the correction with questions like, "What can you do to make sure this is resolved and won't happen again?", "When will you start?", "What do I need to do to help with this?", and "What's the best way to address these issues in the future?"

Overall, the point here is to help the other person grow rather than punish them. They should feel supported and motivated to change their behavior, not depleted and demoralized.

As for yourself, it would be good to think about how you might have contributed to the failure. Had I reflected on my own role with Lisa a bit more, rather than stewing in self-protection, I almost certainly would have noticed my failure to support her properly. And if I had begun our conversation by acknowledging that failure, I would have made her much more comfortable and willing to address her performance.

So a bit of homework before your next feedback meeting can make a big difference. Reflect on what you hope to achieve, and set your intentions. Create a connection that will facilitate change. Often, people feel more comfortable and less self-protective when you admit your faults, if any ("I'm sorry if I didn't support/prepare you well for this program"), and normalize what happened ("We're all human, we all make mistakes and have bad days").

Don't delay the conversations, however difficult they may be. Avoiding them would be a disservice to everyone involved and would only dilute the impact and relevance of your feedback.

Address issues as soon as possible. Giving feedback is not just part of your job, it's something you owe your client. And the way you give feedback, one way or the other, will make a lasting impression.

Giving Recognition and Praise

Now let's address recognition and praise. Giving praise is another essential element in reinforcing positive behavior.

Here are some observations on how constructive comments can help a person's performance and work and highlight the positive aspects of his or her character.

The method of giving recognition and praise touches on two facets: appreciating what they have done and recognizing who they are. In a few words, you are saying 1) "I appreciate your work, project, task, etc." and 2) "I recognize who you are as a person: trustworthy, smart, loyal, punctual, confident, efficient, etc." So, it could sound something like this:

1) "Hey Julie, thank you so much for finishing the project on time and increasing sales. That's an amazing product you created." (The first part appreciates the task that was done.)

2) "I really like how efficient and smart you were in planning and delivering this product." (The second part recognizes them as a person.)

Of course, you need to use your own words—anything that doesn't sound like your own language will be perceived as insincere (because it is). So if your language is something like, "Hey Julie, amazing job on increasing sales this month. You rock at delivering this stuff," so be it. Every business and every department has its own parlance and customs.

Make your words count. Remember that showing appreciation for a task well done is only level one; recognizing the person for who they are is a higher level of acknowledgment. The latter will stick with them longer and will make them feel much more valued. Their projects will change, but their characteristics and qualities will inform their whole career. You could be the person who changed their lives by noticing something in them they hadn't considered.

To further the feeling of recognition and empowerment, you can ask them questions about how they accomplished a given task they're proud of. Ask them to explain, in their own words, what they did and how they achieved their goal. You don't even have to find the right words for recognition; just by being curious and asking them to elaborate on their process, they will realize their talent and see where they need improvement.

One way to have them share is to ask if they would be willing to train or mentor others who need a bit of direction and/or coaching. This is, in my experience, an excellent way to make them feel appreciated while being redirected themselves.

For both constructive and positive feedback, never wait, and offer praise sincerely and often. Sometimes just a thumbs-up, a raised eyebrow, and a smile with a nod can give, as they say, all the recognition in the world.

Questions:

- How often do you offer feedback? Are you waiting for the quarterly reviews or are you sharing frequently?
- How often do you offer direct appreciation and recognition?
- If you think about someone who mentored you, what did they do that was memorable? How can you pay that forward?
- What is your next opportunity to practice this?

Chapter 15

You Need More Empathy; Here Is How to Get It

Learning to see and understand other dancers

Lack of empathy is a serious issue, and yet, very few of us are putting much effort into learning how to become more empathetic. For one, empathy is often pushed aside, replaced by more urgent and quantifiable priorities; often, we simply don't take the time to cultivate empathy because we must focus on deliverables. In some work environments, empathy is even considered an outright obstacle to efficiency and productivity. No wonder so many of us face similar challenges at or outside of work.

Yet it is critical that we weave empathy into our every intention and action, as only through empathy can we positively affect people and create meaningful connections. Empathy is a vital leadership and life skill. Without it, we cannot establish trust, and trust is fundamental to enhancing collaboration and performance.

Research has demonstrated that a lack of empathy affects our mental health and personal lives in the form of stress (due to incivility), and causes high turnover and deteriorating employee engagement at work. On the other hand, innovation, engagement, retention, and inclusivity improve dramatically in organizations where empathy is present.[13] But truly, do we need data and research to prove that a lack of empathy will affect us? Would you want to work in an environment where you didn't feel valued, appreciated, and respected?

Amy lives in the Bay Area. She is a driven and successful leader in the high-tech industry. She has delivered a number of extremely high-profile projects for a number of corporations. During one of our sessions, Amy told me, "I don't know, this stuff is too complicated."

"What stuff?" I asked.

"How to address people," she answered. "We have to be so careful about everything we say. There are so many things to consider, so many personalities. It's exhausting." Then she added, "You know, overall, I don't think

---

[13]"The Power of Empathy in Times of Crisis and Beyond," www.catalyst.org.

I'm that empathetic, and that's probably my problem."

You'd think these might be words from a very young person, but Amy is in her early fifties and has already managed numerous teams. She is known as someone who gets things done.

While she has, overall, a rather pleasant personality, Amy has a way of keeping her ducks in a row, and her team knows this about her. When she talked to me, she would use phrases like, "We don't have time for this fluffy stuff," "Can't they just focus on work? They are paid to do a job," and "I just want to get things done, not be their mother."

Boy, did those words resonate with me! That's exactly how I used to think, and, as a result, I've given my share of insensitive responses. Have you ever talked or thought like Amy? Or used phrases such as "You're too sensitive," "That's just the way I am," or "I don't mean any harm"? If so, you might be in the same boat she was in.

You may argue that this kind of thinking doesn't necessarily show a lack of empathy, but I would encourage you to look a little deeper. At a minimum, I think we could agree that it is a dismissive attitude, and I would argue that whenever we dismiss somebody's personal feelings as irrelevant, we lack empathy.

The big question is whether empathy is a capability that can be trained, developed, and put to good use. And the answer is a resounding yes. We all can develop more empathy, and if we do, we will personally benefit from it just as much as our environment will.

A lack of empathy can stem from a lack of practice and understanding, as well as the culture we live in or were raised in. Some people are naturally more empathetic; others have a harder time picking up cues from others.

What I've learned over the years is that people are people. They have feelings, they get hurt, and they want to be cared for, appreciated, recognized, and viewed for who they are.

For each chapter of this book, for each point I present, empathy is the constant underlying element. It is required when you listen, coach, offer feedback, and delegate, and it's key to how you view yourself and how you "dance."

When I was training to be a Dale Carnegie facilitator, we had to learn specific skills on how to give constructive feedback, show empathy, and make the other person feel good about what they had done so they could improve. For example, when someone gave a three-minute presentation, regardless of how good or awful a job they did, we had to empathize and view their side of the struggle to find something positive to say so they could improve.

During the training, one of the facilitators said, "What's with all the soft words and beating around the bush? Can't we just tell them that what they did was mediocre and guide them to do better?" I remember agreeing with that person at the time. I thought the participants should indeed be able to take in critical feedback and then learn from our guidance. Wasn't that, after all, what we were being paid for? But I've learned since that harsh feedback is no help at all. If we want to inspire and influence someone to achieve a goal, we have to tap into our empathy to connect with the learners in a real and meaningful way.

Not long ago, I watched a social science documentary

on Netflix called *100 Humans.* In one of the experiments, the trainers gave a group of people lessons on how to spin a plate on a stick. Then the trainers let the learners try it out and proceeded to have them perform in front of a panel of judges.

The judges were assigned to randomly give positive or negative feedback to the participants, regardless of their performance. One woman managed to spin the plate for almost a minute. However, she was unknowingly selected to receive negative criticism, despite being one of the best in the group. The judges told her that her performance was terrible. Then the judges gave her some time to go back out and practice again. When she returned, her performance was worse than before. She was unable to spin the plate for more than a few seconds.

Another man, who totally failed and couldn't hold the plate up for a second, was randomly selected to receive a compliment. However hard it was to give positive feedback, the judges found something constructive to say. When he came back for his second round, the man could spin the plate for a few seconds longer. You can see how criticism and lack of empathy can affect performance.

Now, knowing about this experiment, you might think that you can simply give positive feedback and that doing so will automatically lead to positive changes. However, people will sense how genuine you are and soon figure out if the feedback was merely lip service. If you really want feedback to land well, you have to believe that the person indeed has the ability to improve—that there is a chance, however small. Only if you believe that with sincerity will your feedback make people feel seen and heard. This is what empathy means.

So, that's all well and good, but how do we become more empathetic?

While there is no one-size-fits-all approach, several practices can help. The key practice, I believe, is to first pay attention to what you sense and feel and to be aware of your own experiences. We must be self-aware so we can understand what would work for us personally. Now, this kind of awareness does not develop in a vacuum but is honed and tested throughout our life experiences, and some experiences are more likely to foster awareness than others.

I'm going to share with you a few types of experiences that have served to foster my own self-awareness. Ultimately, however, it is up to you to explore and figure out what works best for you. My effort to quantify the impact is obviously only a rough estimate and has certainly varied at different times in my life.

1. Meditation and silence – 10%

2. Travel experiences – 10%

3. Volunteering, especially abroad – 20%

4. Emotional pain and challenging times – 30%

5. Curiosity and listening – 20%

6. Experiencing someone else's life – 10%

1. MEDITATION AND SILENCE– 10%

Much has been written about meditation, but what really happens when you sit in the lotus position trying to quiet your mind? Well, let's start by eliminating that sitting position. Forget that nonsense. Every time I tried the full lotus, my legs fell asleep, my back hurt, and there was more pain than meditation. Now I find it more comfortable to just sit up straight on my sofa. So find out what works for you.

I've been meditating for about thirty years, on and off. I've tried many types of guided meditation to help me quiet my mind, relax, and become centered—for example, focusing on my breathing or my chakras, or doing visualizations. No matter which method I've used, sometimes I've loved meditation and felt a lot more peaceful and calm afterward; other times, I've gotten mad, questioning why I was sitting in the first place and what I was trying to accomplish. Over time, however, I've learned that my mind will quiet down when I've focused long enough on an object—say, my chakras one by one, or on a specific sound around me, or on my breathing, my chest rising and falling, or anything that had a steady beat or regular noise.

But what did meditation bring to me over time? Neuroscientific researchers from Mount Sinai Medical Center in New York City have discovered that when the brain is scanned during meditation, the "empathy" area of the brain (the anterior insular cortex) lights up significantly, and that by calming our nervous system and expanding our inner awareness, we become more aware of our emotions and, therefore, the emotions of others as well.

Indeed, whenever I've been able to get to a place of calm and focus, something has happened in me. Sensing what is within me has helped me notice what is outside of me. By being more aware of my emotions, I've become more sensitive and aware of other people's emotions. Cultivating empathy, I've come to understand, requires exploration, experience, and self-awareness.

Do I know exactly how this breakthrough happened? Not really. But I do know that after meditating regularly for only a few years, I could sense much more of what others were experiencing, probably because I was just more in touch with my own emotions. I began to notice fluctuations in people's moods, energy, and attitude in ways that I wasn't conscious of before. It was like shining a flashlight on my emotions, whether they were anger, joy, fear, excitement, peacefulness, or frustration, and noticing parts of the human condition that had previously been hidden.

In addition to bringing greater focus and understanding, meditation also recentered me. It's like that stone pillar of self I shared in a previous chapter. Especially when doing chakra meditations, for me it was like applying fresh cement to reinforce my pillar of self. When I'm centered, I'm more aware of what I'm sensing internally, which makes me relate more capably and empathically to others.

Do I encourage meditation? Absolutely. I practice meditation a few times a week, sometimes for a full hour, other times for only a few minutes.

See what practices work best for you. Sometimes hiking alone in nature, gardening, working on a puzzle, or painting can help you recenter and connect with your emotions in the same way that formal meditation can. Give it some time and start noticing what happens to you.

2. TRAVEL EXPERIENCES – 10%

I'm a sucker for travel and couldn't live without it. I plan my year around my vacations and jump on any opportunity to explore other cultures.

I grew up in Switzerland, in an Italian family and community. Europeans view vacations differently from Americans. Their vacations last much longer, and they don't hold back on using time off. I used to spend most of my vacations in Italy, then later, I expanded to other countries in Europe. I backpacked solo throughout Southeast Asia, moved to the U.S., volunteered in China and Africa, and continue to travel abroad to this day.

For me, traveling means leaving behind what I am accustomed to and immersing myself in the country and culture I am visiting. It also means discovering how I am affected and reacting to what I experience.

To immerse yourself in the places you visit, the first thing to do is to let go of your world at home. Is that always easy? Lord, no. I used to be so stuck in my comfortable habits that during my travels, sometimes I just didn't like what I was eating, smelling, seeing, or dealing with. But that's part of the immersion and discovery. It is essential to let go of our home customs in order to understand others' cultures. If you are going to be inflexible when abroad, you may as well turn on the Discovery Channel and eat a bowl of cereal on your sofa.

Most importantly, traveling gives you a chance to see how you respond to other cultures. You might uncover other sides of yourself that you didn't know existed. Taking a trip and immersing yourself in a different environment might widen the concept you have of yourself and make you realize that the other person is not really "the other" but a human being similar to you.

Sure, sometimes I want to just be left alone, sit on a beach, and read a book, especially when my vacation time is limited. The point here is to experience something different, something that detaches me from my routines, that gets me in a wholly different mindset. Any experience that allows you to change perspective and get to know yourself a little differently has the potential to increase empathy.

3. VOLUNTEERING, ESPECIALLY ABROAD – 20%

Volunteering is not something I grew up doing. My parents were generous and kind, but they preferred to donate money, not to volunteer. However, while I didn't grow up volunteering, my siblings and I were used to helping family and friends, and we often did so to the point of exhaustion.

Only later in my life did I start volunteering for larger causes, especially abroad, and each of these trips drastically raised my level of empathy. The first time I experienced a considerable jump in compassion from volunteering was when I flew to Ghana as part of a group of volunteers on a medical mission for Alliance for Smiles (AfS).

AfS offers free surgeries across the world for children with cleft lip and cleft palate. On my first mission, I was a quartermaster and sterilizer. I was helping with inventory and was positioned right next to the operating room, sterilizing instruments after each surgery. I also got to help doctors and nurses during intake, and doing so, I saw parents who had traveled for days to bring their children to the hospital. I saw mothers waiting outside of the OR, anxious to see their child's new face after the surgical procedure. I sensed the fathers' concerns and hope. I saw their tears and smiles of joy.

I'll never forget the time my eyes welled up and my throat tightened when a young teenager, Teresa, woke up from surgery, pushed herself up into a sitting position on her recovery room bed, and extended her arms out, wanting to shake everyone's hands. She was so eager to thank us for repairing her face and changing her life. To me, that moment was a seismic one. I was so emotional I had to retreat to the sterilizer room and start cleaning instruments, unable to talk, my tears wetting my surgical mask.

It's moments like the one I had with Teresa that can completely transform you. It's an experience that cracks that hard shell you've carried around for years, opening you up to emotions you've not felt before. But this is a crack that you can't repair and won't wish to either. You want it to keep expanding, growing, and helping you become more authentic, vulnerable, and empathetic. The faces of people you've helped, their looks of appreciation—those are images that stick with you. They have the power to mold a new you.

After Ghana, I went on two similar medical missions to China. One might think you would become somehow more calloused or accustomed to those powerful emotional responses, but it was the opposite. The more in touch I was with my emotions, the more I was touched by my volunteer experiences. I was often overwhelmed just at the sight of families arriving at the hospitals, the faces of parents seeing their children, and then the embraces of gratitude I received. Sometimes it was simple looks of recognition that would fill my heart with compassion.

Acting with empathy is leading by example. It is one thing to understand grief, suffering, or poverty and to have compassion; it's another thing to do something with your empathy.

When you live from your heart, you connect, you blend in, you belong, and you assimilate with your community. You are part of it all rather than looking in from the outside. Additionally, acting out of empathy demonstrates to others how everyday kindness brings out the best of humanity. As a parent, you demonstrate kindness and empathy to your children. As a leader, you merge with your team and organization through empathetic conversations, you become a campfire that people want to sit around and warm themselves by.

4. EMOTIONAL PAIN AND CHALLENGING TIMES – 30%

By no means do I want you to recklessly put yourself into overly challenging situations, nor do I want you to seek out emotional pain, but, as we all know, both are unavoidable and leave a mark. It's what we do with that mark that either helps or stunts our growth.

I believe emotional pain represents up to 30 percent of my growth in empathy because it's in times of pain that I am most vulnerable and sensitive to what others have experienced. Even more important, the memory of the pain reminds me of what it felt like and helps me relate to other people's ordeals.

I can recall numerous painful episodes in my life: moments of solitude during my travels; leaving my family in Europe; separation anxiety; my overwhelming fear of public speaking; the feeling of being an impostor when I applied for a new job or started a new project; failed romantic relationships; the loss of loved ones; the stress of getting married, buying a house, and having a child. Many, if not all, of the big life decisions are exciting in the abstract but can prove terrifying in reality.

Each of these incidents left a mark on me, and these marks helped me become more empathetic. When I encounter someone going through a similar experience, I can better connect with them. I understand that my experience is not the same as theirs, of course, but it will still inform my empathy for them.

When we lack empathy, we might think we are helping others by telling them what to do, to get their act together or to suck it up, and we might think, How can they not resolve XYZ? Talk about approaching someone in the worst possible way!

In a discussion with Brené Brown, David Kessler once pointed out that anytime we are judging somebody, we are, in effect, punishing that person. I agree and I know that, unfortunately, I have at times done so myself. My tone of voice, facial expressions, and arguments were implicitly "grading" people and their actions according to scale, which is to say, I judged them.

All too often we tend to compare suffering and pain

according to our own gauge, but the pain that someone is experiencing is theirs alone and is sometimes impossible to assess. A child crying about a broken toy is not helped by being told, "Oh, come on, it's only a toy," just as much as you wouldn't want to have someone say, "Oh come on, it's just your sixty-thousand-dollar car that was totaled."

Your experience of pain is yours alone and is in accordance with your current capacities and circumstances. "The worst loss is always *your* loss," Kessler pointed out. But if you believe that the loss of a five-dollar toy and a sixty-thousand-dollar car are incomparable, you are in judgment; you are using your scale to evaluate a child's loss against an adult's.

True empathy means feeling the other's pain without judgment.

5. CURIOSITY AND LISTENING – 20%

Being curious about what you sense and paying attention to your emotions, triggers, and physical or emotional discomfort will enhance your growth and help you become more empathetic. Paying attention and exploring what happens within you will inform you of what is happening outside of you. Why?

It is like sampling a new dish. When you focus on the taste buds in your mouth or the olfactory cells in your nose, you better understand the food's texture, flavor, taste, and smell. Observing how your senses respond to that first bite is comparable to listening to your emotions as they are unfolding. If we observe with curiosity and an open mind, we will enrich our understanding of others and become more empathetic.

One simple way to practice empathy through curiosity and listening is to talk to people you don't talk to very often: a neighbor, a colleague from another department, a member of a club you belong to. Go to a location you typically don't visit, like a different building, or a neighborhood you don't usually go to. Strike up a conversation with the passenger next to you on the bus or the plane. Be curious and listen . . . and see what happens. Are you triggered by their ways of living, thoughts, or culture? Are you easily judging or grading them? If so, is it because you are not listening well and being curious?

6. EXPERIENCE SOMEONE ELSE'S LIFE – 10%

When I interviewed customers to learn how they wanted me to develop a software application for them, or when I shadowed someone for a few hours to better understand their work and its challenges, it was always eye-opening for me to experience their life, to put myself in their shoes.

The television series *Undercover Boss* is an excellent example of what experiencing someone's work or life is like, and you can do the same without adopting a disguise. Instead, you can ask to spend time with people you want to understand. In my experience, after I have spent time with clients and learned what their jobs and lives are like, I feel welcomed into their world. If you are a project manager or anyone who is part of a development life cycle, you already know that your best chance of understanding someone is to spend time with them, be curious, and ask questions.

Experiencing someone else's life means leaving aside what you feel, even if it's just for a moment, and putting yourself in the other person's shoes, feeling what this person feels. Research[14] shows that when we experience someone else's life, mirror neurons fire up and we are literally "mirroring" the other person. You may have experienced something similar when you felt joy in seeing a person succeed or recoiled in pain when watching an accident in a video.

When you fully take in someone's grief, you are more likely to empathize and support that person. Doing so will often also create the space for you to become more vulnerable with them; as a result, you are creating opportunities for others to show empathy toward you. Such greater fluidity will almost certainly lead to a much-improved relationship.

Like everything else, empathy grows with practice. It's easy to revert to being self-centered, especially when you feel triggered by fear or stress. The real work, I think, lies in honing our ability to catch ourselves in those moments. It is only when we are not caught up in our emotion that we can expand our horizon to see the other side.

Despite my own progress in this area, there are still times when I might react unskillfully, without empathy. The six points above have helped me tremendously, but at times I might still get annoyed at somebody. If that happens, at least I now have enough awareness to walk away before I say something I'll regret. Growing your empathy

[14]A.D. Baird, I.E. Scheffer, and S.J. Wilson, "Mirror neuron system involvement in empathy: A critical look at the evidence," https://www.tandfonline.com/doi/abs/10.1080/17470919.2010.547085.

is a process that is never done, that never comes to an end. Every interaction offers us a new opportunity to practice. While this process is never finished, I do know that when I look in the mirror today, I know that I am no longer the person I used to be. I believe I have become a better person, a more understanding person. The key to that is empathy.

Questions:

- How do you feel when people around you are feeling sad?
- Before criticizing someone, how often do you try to put yourself in their shoes?
- Is it easy or difficult for you to sense what makes someone you know happy?
- Is it upsetting to you when someone is treated disrespectfully?
- Were there times when you could have been more empathetic? Why weren't you?
- Which of the above six elements have you tried? Which one could you spend more time doing?

Part 3

Creating Your Own Dance

Whatever happens to us happens *for* us; it's the confusion and challenges that give us perspective, depth, and the opportunity for transformation.

When facing new challenges, however, we often revert to habitual responses that feel safe in the moment. What if instead we had strategies to anticipate and embrace challenges for their growth potential? What if we had a higher vision of ourselves strong enough to shed our fears and become self-determined? What if we could respond to every new challenge with the flexibility and fluidity of a great dancer? It is then that we would truly become the leaders we were born to be. We would no longer dance to somebody else's tune but to the music that is in us.

Chapter 16

Off the Dance Floor and Onto the Balcony

Where are you dancing?

"Sam," I said, "I need to ask you something. You've been telling me that your schedule is full, that you are jumping from one task and meeting to another and find yourself exhausted at 6:00 p.m., is that right?"

"Yes," he replied, "but I also relax from time to time during the day."

"OK, great. And what do you do to relax?"

Without hesitation, Sam answered, "I code, fix bugs

in programs . . . things like that."

"Sorry," I said, "it's 6:00 p.m., you've had a full day, you're tired, and your idea of relaxing is going home and coding?"

"Yes," he said. "Coding, for me, is like going back to the cradle, it's my 'brain candy.' I can focus on solving a problem or find a new way to apply a process. It's my 'me' time." He continues, "When I can just sit in front of the computer with an idea and no one to talk to, creating something new, then after an hour I compile the code, and I see it working, oh boy, it's just so special, I feel great."

I could relate. I remember my days of coding and how much I enjoyed such moments of creativity. There is something so rewarding and relaxing about it. Even today, in my current work, I enjoy the times I can create some formulas in a spreadsheet.

When you work on something you love, you tune out everything else—other people, your worries, the chatter in your head. Whether it's the medical field, construction, manufacturing, or high-tech, clients have told me about having similarly soothing moments. You are returning to the basics, to what got you into the job in the first place.

Now, as enjoyable as these "back to the cradle" moments are, getting pulled back into these sorts of tasks can create issues—especially if you are in management. Let's look at how it affected Sam and his team.

Sam was a manager of engineering with a team of eight. Because he loved his old part of the job so much (coding), he got continuously pulled into small engineering matters, filling up his calendar with issues that distracted him from his current managerial role. Anytime someone had a problem, they would come to him for advice and solutions. Because he liked being the problem solver and getting his hands on the code, he would jump in and help without hesitation, collaborating with his team to find an answer. Sometimes, he ended up doing the work himself. He was the problem solver. He was the hero. Bravo!

Well, not so much. If you are in a position similar to Sam's, I am sorry to break it to you: you're not much of a hero at all. In fact, you are damaging your role as leader to your reports and your organization. There are two main pitfalls for leaders. One is operating in reactive mode, always putting out fires. The other is acting like a knowledge hoarder, taking away people's opportunities to grow. Both will hold you back in your leadership role.

Rather than being pulled down into the weeds, let's look at how you can operate in a creative stance, from the "balcony."

Being in Reactive Mode

So many people I talk to want to advance in their careers yet they are so tied to putting out fires and being in the weeds that they continue to operate in reactive mode. They are pulled into the "details" because they have built an identity on such tasks and they love being in the limelight—the hero, the savior. You can get a kick out of being in that stance, but that's the first thing you need to stop doing if you want to become a more efficient leader.

Operating in a reactive mindset will force you to continue addressing situations by removing what you don't want, what doesn't work, or what needs to be fixed: problems, risks, barriers, glitches. You are in damage control, right and left.

When we operate in this mode, we react to situations instead of anticipating them. We fall into avoidance and consider it normalcy. It's a vicious loop that keeps us in a pattern of 1) noticing a challenge or obstacle, 2) feeling the anxious need to fix it, 3) resolving the problem, and 4) feeling relief when the problem is fixed.

These four steps make us want to react and address the challenges right away. As a result, over time, it's like riding a wave with ups and downs, where the bottom of the waves represents the problems and the anxiety to resolve them (points 1 and 2) and the crest of the waves is the resolutions and the satisfaction in fixing them (points 3 and 4). This wave gets us to continuously react to challenges and move from stressed to hero multiple times a day or week, which is an exhausting, addictive cycle.

Don't get me wrong, there is nothing wrong with wanting to resolve problems. But if you're going to be a leader, you have to move away from ongoing problem solving and maintenance and, instead, get into a creative mindset and a new way of operating. Too often, we think that we can resolve issues by just removing hurdles, and yet, the better approach would be to go upstream and create a new pathway that will help us avoid continuous maintenance.

To move from a reactive to a creative and upstream stance means that we must drastically change the way we think. Let me give you an example. Say you are developing an application to allow people to view a store's inventory in your town. As you develop the application, you will have to analyze all the possible obstacles users could encounter and understand how people might use your app. You'll anticipate what they want, the shopping trends, the pain points buyers might experience, and the store's advantages/disadvantages. When you go through this process, you are operating upstream in a creative mode. You analyze, design, code, and build your product in a creative stance so you'll avoid having to react to problems with fear and anxiety.

Now, what's interesting here is that we can efficiently operate in that creative mode when developing our products. Still, we fail to function in a creative way when we need to build ourselves into leaders. And yet, it's just the same. When talking with Sam, I wanted him to start thinking about what his days would look like if he could liberate himself from having to deal with fires all the time. I asked, "What would you do if you could free up space in your calendar?" He answered, "I could start strategizing more and focus on higher-level endeavors."

Exactly: like building an application, we need to strategize and do the research before we even start coding and developing algorithms. We first need to concentrate on the vision. We have to adopt a mindset where the focus is not on what we do not want but on envisioning a positive outcome for us and our respective teams.

Indeed, for Sam to move away from that tendency to put

out fires continuously, he needs to apply this same mindset. He needs to focus on creating what matters. He will have to spend time reflecting on what he wishes to realize for his team and organization, rather than dwelling on what he wants to avoid. He will come to realize what matters as he reflects on what motivates him intrinsically, and he can then take steps to materialize his vision as a leader. Now, let's look at the second pitfall.

When Hoarding Knowledge Prevents People's Growth

There is great satisfaction in being a hero. Who doesn't want to save the day? There is, however, a fine line between doing so in a way that allows other people to resolve their own issues and becoming the sole solution provider. When you do all the work yourself, you may gain and even become addicted to the recognition you receive. Consequently, without that recognition, you might experience resentment or stress, or feel sorry for yourself. I named this the "Hero Syndrome"—that unconscious necessity to be needed and valued, which creates bitterness when not validated.

People operating in this mode often become insecure information hoarders. They hold on to knowledge because they fear that if they release it or let others share it, they will lose power and their perceived worth.

Such people say things like, "Well, if I tell them how to do this and delegate the task, then what am I here for? They may as well get rid of me." I've heard this sentiment expressed many times. It's important to recognize that such thoughts come from a place of scarcity and fear. This mindset holds you back from developing yourself as a leader and deters others from developing into competent and independent contributors. Being an information hoarder creates an environment of dependency where people are held back from fully developing their potential and will continue to rely on others to solve their issues.

When I mentioned these points to Sam, he could easily recognize himself in this behavior. He realized he was not spending enough time developing his team and strategizing on higher-level planning.

While he fully understood the issue, he brought up a point that was challenging for him. "Roberto," he said, "if I want to create more space on my calendar to strategize, I have to start saying no to people. That's not easy for me." I understood, after years of saying yes to everything myself, he couldn't just turn around and deny every request that came his way.

So we discussed other ways he could respond to his team when asked for help. I invited him to create a list with all the tasks and conversations he participated in. Next I asked him to identify which of these many tasks he was uniquely capable of solving and which could be handled by others.

I asked him to grab a piece of paper, draw a line down the middle, and create two columns. Feel free to do the same for yourself right now. Title the first column "My areas of expertise"; in this column, write down what you, in your role, are uniquely able to provide. Then, title the second column "Tasks I can delegate"; here, write down all the tasks, projects, conversations, or meetings you regularly work on that could be done by someone else.

If you do this exercise honestly, you will likely find no more than five items in the first column and many more (everything else) in the second column. The second column is the one that keeps you in reactive mode (in the weeds), the one that ultimately stops you from dancing on the balcony. You need to start saying no to the items in your "Tasks I can delegate" column.

Of course, you are not truly saying no to the second column; rather, you are building people up so that they can problem solve on their own. You are not there to micromanage, doing other people's work coding, but to support and empower others. If you offer the right support in the right language, over time, your reports will leave you alone, and you can spend time focusing on your areas of expertise.

For now, I'll ask you to start shifting from a hoarder mindset to one that provides you the discipline to say no and the resilience around possibly disappointing others.

If you're a parent, you'll know exactly what it feels like when you hold back saying yes to someone you care about. You've probably experienced a time when you saw your child facing a challenging moment and all you wanted to do was help, but you also knew that if you did that, you'd deprive them of the opportunity to learn and grow on their own. So, you stay on the sidelines in distress and watch them struggle because you know they need to go through the pain to move into the world on their own someday.

So it is with your team at work. Think for a moment.

How many times have you telephoned a colleague to help you with a problem, and when they didn't answer the phone, you went back at it and found a solution on your own? Then, when they called, you said, "Ah, no worries, I figured it out"?

Restraining yourself from jumping in every time your collaborators think they need help will, over time, be far more rewarding for you because you will know that you have contributed to their growth, even if you were not directly involved in the process. Truly, that is being a hero and a leader. Once you realize that the world can go on without your constant involvement, you will experience a much greater freedom and be able to realize your vision for the future.

What It's Like to Dance on the Balcony

Sam was making a lot of progress.

In between our sessions, he applied what we discussed and started to implement his new leadership style. The requests kept coming in, and he would reflect on each of them and decide whether to say yes or no. He admitted that it was difficult for him to say no, not only because he didn't like doing so but also because he had to hold back the urge to satisfy his hero identity.

As the weeks went by, he started to become less involved, and his calendar was less crammed. He shared his screen with me and showed me his weekly schedule. "Do you see all these green boxes?" he asked. "They are all new blocks of free time." We counted them. He had fourteen green boxes for that week alone; before, he'd had none.

"So, tell me," I said. "What are you going to do with all these new boxes?" He looked at me and said, "Well, that's what I want to talk about today." He then shared that he was still spending a lot of time checking in on his people, micromanaging, and he didn't like that. It didn't feel right to him. As we talked, he realized that he continued to be involved because he felt the need to be busy and fill his time—fill the green boxes with old habits.

Transitioning to a new leadership style can be difficult, and it was perfectly normal for Sam to experience this type of compensation during his "phases of transition." William Bridges, author of *Managing Transitions*, defined three stages of this process:

1. **Ending, Losing, and Letting Go:** This first stage is marked by resistance and emotional upheaval. Nobody enjoys being required to do something that is uncomfortable and evokes fear, denial, anger, and sadness.

2. **The Neutral Zone:** In the second stage, people are often confused, impatient, and uncertain. Here they might experience resentment toward change, low morale and productivity, anxiety about their roles, and skepticism. This stage can create more work because people are still handling old systems while moving into new ones.

3. **The New Beginning:** In this last stage, people experience acceptance and a boost of energy. They start to embrace changes and have built the requisite skills. Now, they see more "wins," open up to change, and feel more committed to learning.

Bridges explains that people go through each stage at their own pace. The evolution will happen faster if it's a comfortable change, and slower with more difficult transitions.

When I coach clients and note their ambivalence to transition, I use an exercise that helps them consider the risks of changing. I ask a series of "What could happen if/then?" questions that will help them change their thinking. You are probably familiar with this line of inquiry, as you might already use it when evaluating opportunities for your programs or plans. If you find yourself in doubt about changing your leadership style, I suggest you do this exercise as well.

Here is how a session went with Sam.

When he described how counterproductive it was to say yes to too many requests, I would ask, "What would happen if you said no?"

"I feel like I might not be valued anymore for my work," he said. I then asked, "What might happen then?"

"Well, if I'm not valued, I'm not going to have a job any longer."

To this, I just paused and allowed for silence, then asked, "How likely is it that you'll lose your job?"

He looked at me and smiled. "Truth is, there is no way

that would happen." He recognized he was being irrational.

So I asked again, "Then what could really happen if you said no?"

He sat back in his chair, threw his hands in the air, and said, "You know what, I think it's just me resisting change, and I'm afraid of things that don't exist."

Sam and I were getting somewhere. Now I needed to apply the same questions but in reverse, looking at what could happen if Sam did the opposite. So I said, "OK, we just looked at your old ways, and we could see how they made you act. Now let's explore what could happen if you adopted a new behavior, one that is in alignment with who you want to be and what you want to achieve."

When you do this exercise, I encourage you to go with your first thought and response, even if it might seem a bit ridiculous. When done well, this practice helps you see your own illusions, how you are trapped in a habitual cycle, in your own Catch-22. You'll realize that if you don't change and you continue with your old hero leadership style, your schedule will remain packed, you'll continue to be exhausted at the end of the day, and you'll be of little use to yourself or to your organization.

As we went on with our conversation, I also asked Sam, "Is there an issue of trust? Is this why you are checking in on them?" He answered, "No, in fact, because I've changed my language with them, they are more autonomous and move forward without my help."

"So, what else could it be?" I asked.

He thought about it for a moment and then said, "Hmm,

I think it's because now I have no more excuses not to work on my strategies and my actual role."

Exactly. That is a very common reaction, and I was happy that Sam discovered it. Once you have removed all the obstacles to what you are "uniquely" qualified for and in charge of delivering, you must face the music and start dancing.

For Sam, that meant spending time in meetings with upper management and then collaborating with his peers and other teams to fulfill the company's needs. He needed to be out of the weeds and on the balcony to get a wider view of what lay ahead.

Now, to be clear, saying no and being on the balcony doesn't mean detaching from your team. In fact, you must stay in touch with your crew and walk the fields. Like Sam had learned to do, he regularly grabbed members of his team, one by one, and brought them to the balcony so they, too, could have a better view of the company plans. Offering your team access to your plans is crucial because it helps them understand how vital their roles are in achieving them. The more they realize how their work contributes to the big picture, the more engaged they are in their career and personal growth. Supporting them in their contributions is key to your leadership role.

Questions:

- What is your "brain candy," your go-to when you want to relax?
- Are you spending more time in the weeds or on the balcony?

- What drags you down? What would it take to spend more time on the balcony?
- In what mode are you primarily operating, reactive or creative mode? Why?

In their book *Scaling Leadership*, Anderson and Adams identified ten tendencies of people working in reactive or creative modes. As you can see, there is quite a difference between the two styles, and I encourage you to honestly assess what characteristics apply to you.

REACTIVE 10
Ineffective Interaction Style
Not a Team Player
Team Not Fully Developed
Over-Demanding
Micromanages
Team Not Held Accountable
Inattentive/Poor Listener
Too Self-Centered
Lacks Emotional Control
Impatient

CREATIVE 10
Strong People Skills
Vision
Team-Building Skills
Personality/Approachability
Leads by Example
Passionate & Driven

Good Listener
Develops People
Empowers People
Positive Attitude

Chapter 17

Planning Your Self-Transformation

Choreograph your own dance

The Australian psychiatrist W. Béran Wolfe summed up his philosophy like this: "If you observe a really happy man, you will find him building a boat, writing a symphony, educating his son, growing double dahlias in his garden, or looking for dinosaur eggs in the Gobi Desert."

Happiness research has demonstrated that people who are engaged in something that is of personal significance to them—whether learning a new skill, changing professions, or raising a family—are far happier than those who live life without a vision or ambition.

When you find a happy person, you are also finding a *project*.

Happiness is not just an endpoint, a final state of mind you want to reach; it is a process.

If I asked you to reflect on the accomplishments you are most proud of, you would probably find that it was truly the *process* of achieving them that made you feel alive and engaged. Even if you ran into some headaches and had to adjust the process many times, those hurdles were all part of what kept you passionate and focused on your goal.

Going through self-transformation requires a similar approach. You'll have to be fluid, knowing that you'll encounter difficult moments and will need to adapt your route while you simultaneously remain involved in reaching your goals.

So, what is the best way to achieve self-transformation? As for all the projects you've worked on before, you'll need a plan. You'll have to define a clear method to attain your objective.

I will help you design such a plan in this chapter. But before we get there, let's reflect on what you want to accomplish in your self-transformation. Start asking yourself the following questions:

- What are the fundamental pain points you are currently experiencing?
- What are people telling you about areas in which you need to improve?

• What are some recurring challenges you face related to the subjects I've addressed in this book?

The better you can identify these core points, the easier it will be to create a plan for self-growth. And, most importantly, with a plan, you'll increase your chances of overcoming obstacles and address arguments and concerns that could get in the way of your objectives. Without a plan, you won't get to your destination.

I like to plan. I've done it for years while developing applications and managing projects. Even when I travel, although I remain flexible along the way, I plan for eventual problems so they won't preclude me from enjoying my trip.

For example, I decided to ride my motorcycle solo across Mexico a few years ago. Before I left, I shared my plans with my friends and coworkers. Invariably, they said things like, "You're crazy! People are getting killed, it's too dangerous," and "It's not safe to travel solo around Mexico, especially on a motorcycle," and "You must be out of your mind!"

They all raised scary points and possibilities about Mexico; the shootings, the thefts, the cartels, the dangerous regions, the peril of traveling alone on my motorcycle. Their comments didn't fall on deaf ears.

Some of my friends were trying to dissuade me from going, but I had a detailed plan to anchor myself. I had already spent hours designing my itinerary, mapping out my route to avoid sketchy areas and addressing possible motorcycle issues.

Likewise, for your self-transformation, you will require

solid planning so you can stay true to your objectives, know how to face challenges, and find support when needed.

With most of my clients, after we finish their 360-feedback review, I ask them to create a plan for their leadership growth. In the plan, I ask them to define key objectives that they want to achieve. They have to consider the feedback they receive, their leadership style when achieving their goals, and what specific points they want to work on.

The plan also needs to include check-ins with people who will be involved in the process; this is necessary so that my clients hold themselves accountable and receive feedback as they progress. A plan that provides for all these elements will keep them focused along the way.

There are two tools that have proven extremely helpful in laying the foundation for the process: the Development Action Plan (DAP) and the Motivation and Transformation Quadrant (MTQ). (Both templates are part of a workbook you can find on my website at www.giannicola.com.)

Development Action Plan (DAP)

The Development Action Plan will address four points:

1. Your character strengths and values. How do people describe you? What are the first few words that they use? What are your strengths and weaknesses? As suggested earlier, you can ask people directly, use a character strength finder website, or explore your strengths and values by yourself.

It's essential to identify your character strengths and values in your plan because we don't want to focus only on areas in need of improvement. Include the qualities that make you who you are and that would best represent your "brand." Your strengths are your most important tools that will help you improve. For example, if you are described as a person with grit, loyalty, intelligence, and an entrepreneurial spirit, these are characteristics that you can leverage to attain your goals and address your weak points.

2. How do you show up at your lowest and highest?
How do you behave when you are under stress? When you are triggered? When you are operating at low levels (e.g., when you are at your worst, not following your values, having a bad day)? Conversely, how do you behave when you perform at your highest level (e.g., highly engaged, enthusiastic, driven)? How do people react to you?

Also reflect on what gets you down versus what energizes you to be more efficient, driven, and engaged. Understanding your highs and lows is important in that it will help you anticipate your responses to best inform your behavior.

3. Choose three main objectives—at most! When developing project plans, don't put too many goals in the same proposal. Similarly, start with the foundational work, then add components and build up section by section. You must break down the areas you want to develop, create milestones, and not overwhelm yourself with too many aspects of your self-transformation. A multitude of objectives will render your plan unachievable and set you up for failure.

I ask my clients to select the top three objectives they want to focus on, no more than three. They'll have to define them as Objective 1, Objective 2, and Objective 3.

Each objective will need to include:

1) What you are planning on changing
2) How you plan on making that change
3) What others should observe about you as a result of achieving your objective
4) What you want to experience for yourself as a result of this change

Additionally, I ask them to envision a Final Resolution. This is the overall outcome of their endeavors. For example, suppose their Objective 1 is to become a better communicator. In that case, the result might be that they can influence their reports to feel more empowered and handle more work independently, which in turn will give them more time to strategize.

The Final Resolution could be higher productivity, more sales, and/or reduced expenses for the organization. By letting everyone understand how your transformation will support the Final Resolution in terms of revenue, productivity, innovation, etc., and the benefits to your organization, you'll find additional motivators and support for your journey.

4. Support and accountability partners. You'll have to think about what type of support you plan to include in your transformation. Here is what I suggest:

- **Get feedback:** Consult with peers, reports, family members, friends—anyone who can give you feedback about your interpersonal style, telling you what you are doing well and what could still improve.

- **Ask a mentor:** Find a person who is already good at the skills you want to improve. It doesn't have to be the same person for each objective. Think of someone you already admire for how he/she uses these skills. Talk to them. Ask if they can support you.

- **Work with a coach:** If your organization offers coaching, take advantage of it. A certified professional coach can help you make progress and help you reflect on what is important for you to change.

- **Sign up for a workshop:** There are many programs you can attend, in person or online, that are offered for free by your company. Take advantage of them, particularly if they are live and allow you to role-play and practice with other participants.

- **Practice in the workplace:** Have a facilitator/consultant conduct a group practice with all your collaborators to understand and share more about what behaviors you can improve, expectations, and agreements. Additionally, implement and challenge yourself with the skills you want to improve by practicing them in your meetings, one-on-one conversations, facilitating groups, etc.

- **Keep an awareness journal:** Create a practice of daily or weekly check-ins to review your progress. Reflect on your day and think about times when you did well or could have done better. Without judging or being hard on yourself, notice and make it a point to improve.

As you can see, the structure of a DAP for self-transformation is somewhat like a plan for a technical project. The content is different, but it includes milestones, meetings, consultation with external providers, and weekly logs/check-ins to measure your work's progress.

Finally, the DAP will work best if you are comfortable sharing it. You don't need to give people all the details; a summary of your DAP usually suffices. Let them know that you are trying to improve specific skills and would appreciate their support and feedback.

I've coached clients who felt reluctant to share their plans with coworkers because they believed they would be judged or appear weak. The truth is, if you feel that way, you might want to include building confidence and understanding vulnerability and authenticity into your plan.

I've yet to meet someone who didn't benefit from sharing a plan. When sharing, people usually receive encouragement, peers in turn share their challenges, and, as a result, they create even stronger connections. Seeking feedback can be as simple as asking a colleague to comment on how you addressed a situation or how you spoke or presented an argument. The more transparency you have while working through your DAP, the stronger the connections and the more supported you will be in achieving your goals.

When I planned my trip to Mexico, I was motivated to design the journey following my vision and my yearning to experience something wonderful. Likewise, the motivation behind what you want to achieve in your self-transformation needs to be uniquely yours.

Why do I say this? I've worked with clients who started putting together a Development Action Plan to only respond to what other people asked them to improve. But focusing only on external feedback omits a crucial element: what you, intrinsically, are motivated to develop for yourself. So take the time to reflect on your vision; otherwise, it would be like planning a trip you take only to satisfy your friends. Who is going on this trip, you or your friends?

Motivation and Transformation Quadrant (MTQ)

In order to reflect on and better understand your achievement motivations, you need to create a Motivation and Transformation Quadrant (MTQ).

This quadrant asks you to reflect on four points: Yourself; Your Business or Career; Your Clients or Beneficiaries; and the World and Your Community. Grab a large sheet of paper and write these four titles at the top of each quadrant. Then, take time to reflect and write bullet points in each box about the kind of transformation you want to experience. Answer each of the following questions:

1. **Yourself:** What transformation do you want for yourself as a result of achieving your goals?

2. Your Business or Career: What transformation do you want for your business or career as a result of achieving your goals?

3. Your Clients or Beneficiaries: What transformation do you want your colleagues, clients, or the people receiving your services to experience as a result of working with you as you achieve your goals?

4. The World and Your Community: What transformation do you want your goal or services to inspire or change in the world and community?

It is best if you work on this quadrant with a pen and paper instead of typing it. Many studies suggest that there are brain-friendly and creative benefits to writing by hand.

As you answer these questions, you're going to gain clarity about your purpose and personal transformation. It's this Motivation and Transformation Quadrant, in addition to your Development Action Plan, that will keep you on the correct path.

OK, you're all good and ready to work on your plan, but how will you know you are making progress? That's often a tricky question, because soft skills like communication, listening, coaching, and empathy are somewhat intangible aptitudes.

But here are a couple of ways that my clients have known they were on track with their plans:

1) People tell you without telling you. You will notice that people around you become closer and more relatable. They will start asking you questions. They'll share more and ask you to be involved in projects or meetings you were excluded from before.

Mostly, you'll see an external positive change in how people engage with you. Trust will increase among your team, and, because of that, you'll notice more collaboration. Overall, the rapport you have with everyone will improve.

2) You won't behave the same way. You'll notice that you feel more centered and less frazzled by external events. You'll feel more emotionally connected with people and will know how to remain balanced and focused.

You'll worry less and feel more entrepreneurial. You'll respond to requests with more optimism and feel confident about future results. You'll be able to relate more easily with others, feel more empathy, and connect with them more genuinely.

You will be "in flow" and realize where you feel and perform at your best. Your sense of self will disappear, and you will be in motion with everyone and everything, increasing performance and results.[15]

Now that you know about the importance of creating a DAP and an MTQ, I would like you to know that this is not always going to be easy. Like any endeavor, there is often a lot of drive and excitement at the outset, but, with time,

---

[15]Steven Kotler, "Frequently Asked Questions on Flow," stevenkotler.com, 2020.

hurdles appear, and our enthusiasm wanes. So you need to know how to overcome your doubts and prepare for fatigue.

I've experienced such moments of doubt frequently. After planning my trip to Mexico for several months, on the day of departure, I woke up with a pit in my stomach. Was I crazy to go on this trip? What if my friends were right about the dangers? I didn't want to linger on these thoughts, so I got up and pushed my worries aside. By nine in the morning, I said goodbye to my daughter, got on my motorcycle, and pulled out of my driveway, aiming south.

On day two, I crossed the border and arrived in Puerto Peñasco, just as planned. After checking in to my hotel, I went out to get some dinner. I strolled along the ocean. The sun was setting and it was a bit windy. A group of teenagers was sitting on a wall by the beach; I could hear them laughing. Seagulls floated over the horizon. I was watching the sun disappearing in the ocean, standing alone, hands in my pocket, under red skies. It could have been a perfect moment, beautiful and serene. Except it wasn't. Instead, it hit me: "What the hell am I doing here? What am I trying to prove to myself? This is freaking ridiculous!"

I was questioning my whole trip and thinking of canceling everything and turning around. I can drive back home tomorrow, I thought. What am I doing this for?

Then I fell silent. I knew the Green Monster was trying to take over. Trying to calm down, I walked back to town, stopped at a local restaurant, and ordered a beer and a few tacos. About thirty minutes later, I saw a motorcyclist pull over across the street. He walked into a restaurant across the street and sat down. I watched him set up his smartphone on a tripod in front of him. He pressed a button and started talking. Probably one of those vloggers traveling the world with a YouTube channel, I thought.

I paid my bill, walked across the street, and began talking to the guy. I was right; he was a vlogger from Spain who had been traveling for over ten years on his own. "I don't even have a home anymore," he said. He shared his experience, and I later found him on the Internet.

Our conversation immediately restored my enthusiasm for the trip. I've traveled alone many times before, and he reminded me of how enriching that is. The next day, I woke up excited to get back on the road, and I continued my trip farther south. Worries continued to come up occasionally, but each time I made a conscious effort to acknowledge the Green Monster and let it pass.

My strategy worked. By the end of the first week, most of my worries were behind me and the beauty of Mexico lay ahead to explore.

No doubt, you'll have plenty of moments like I had. When they come up, you'll have to tap into your growth mindset. Self-transformation is a bold undertaking, but it is not unachievable. Take note of small progress and celebrate your wins. As you move forward, embrace changes as elements of your development.

And when you have doubts and the Green Monster arrives, talk through these obstacles so you can cast them aside and create space for something else to help you. You'll be surprised by what support shows up. Just be patient and have faith.

The second pitfall to be prepared for is fatigue (i.e., mental blocks or burnout).

Want to know how many times I ran into mental blocks and fatigue while writing this book? Don't get me started. This is my first book, and yes, I launched into this effort by beginning with a Development Action Plan and a Motivation and Transformation Quadrant. I've also created a Mind Map of all the subjects I wanted to write about. The same way I tackle most of my projects, I was engaged full force for the first few months and produced a ton of work.

But then came the revisions, the restructuring, more ideas to implement, and more reviews. I was overwhelmed by how many facets of writing a book I had to consider. I started to procrastinate and experience mental fatigue, resulting in a lack of drive. That's when I realized I had to take a pause. I was becoming an obstruction to my book and even started to forget why I was writing it in the first place.

The first and probably most crucial step was to realize what was happening to me: I was exhausted and blocked. The second part was to take a pause. I began to implement frequent short breaks to help me focus on something other than the mental strain of working closely with a text. This required getting into my body and doing physical things like gardening, hiking, exercise, or repairs around my home—manual work. This second step provided brief periods of relief from my mental fatigue by shifting to more kinesthetic activities.

I also began to take longer breaks. I went on short three- to four-day vacations. I left all my work behind and enjoyed my time away. I went camping in the wilderness and took a few motorcycle trips. The point was to ease up the intense focus and allow for creativity to be restored. When you do that, a natural reawakening will occur, and you'll think and feel much more refreshed, with new ideas in your mind.

Finally, I reminded myself of the purpose of writing this book. I revisited my points in the Motivation and Transformation Quadrant and the impact that this work can have. I needed to reconnect with my purpose.

Likewise, remember why *you* are working on your self-transformation and what it could look like once you reach your goals.

It is key that we know how to reset and reenergize ourselves. You can experiment with the factors that worked for me, but make sure you build your own toolbox to overcome doubt and fatigue in your self-transformation.

Science explains that only 8 percent of people achieve their goals. The reason these people do succeed, according to the research,[16] is that they practice and follow key elements:

• Begin with the end in mind

• Build a support system

• Set specific and challenging (but not too hard) goals

• Stay passionate and committed to the end

• Get feedback

• Avoid multitasking

---

[16]University of Scranton, Inc.com, "Science Says 92 Percent of People Don't Achieve Their Goals," https://www.inc.com/marcel-schwantes/science-says-92-percent-of-people-dont-achieve-goals-heres-how-the-other-8-perce.html.

To that list, I would add, "Have fun with it." I've made the mistake of being too rigid with myself, without adding fun and rewarding experiences to my plan. I'd recommend letting go of such rigidity and allowing for some space to breathe and make mistakes.

Three weeks into my motorcycle trip across Mexico, I was riding north from Zihuatanejo to Manzanillo. An hour after I started my journey, I was caught in a thunderstorm. In minutes, I was completely drenched. I decided to pull over and take cover under the large awning of a grocery store.

The owner of the store, a man named Miguel, was sitting out front. When he saw me, he grabbed another chair and invited me to sit down. In the hour waiting for the storm to pass, we talked about life and business. I saw his children and his store. Miguel was curious, caring, and heartwarming.

He insisted on sending me off with some empanadas his wife had made. Then I drove off and continued riding north along the beautiful coastal road. The air was damp from the storm, and as the sun came out, I could smell the jungle that stretched along one side of the road, and the blue ocean on the other. I rode the curvy road while listening to soft music through the speakers in my helmet.

And then something happened: my eyes welled up, and I was suddenly overwhelmed with joy. Everything was just perfect: the road, the music, Miguel, the weather, all blended together to offer me one of the most memorable days of my trip.

My plan had come true.

Sometimes you'll wonder why you took on this journey of self-transformation, and perhaps, sometimes, you'll want to throw in the towel. Don't quit; keep looking at your map. The struggles and difficulties are part of the voyage, and, step by step, you'll realize that it was all worth it.

Now, go create your plan!

Questions:

- What are the points that you know about yourself that need to be addressed?
- Do you have a plan for your own life and career? What's in it?
- What will keep you on track? What would you write in your Motivation and Transformation Quadrant that would keep you on task?

Chapter 18

Stuck Between a Hammer and a Cappuccino

Nothing happens unless you step onto the dance floor

"A ship in harbor is safe, but that is not what ships are built for." —*John Augustus Shedd*

We do so many things in our life—some easy and mundane, others difficult and seemingly out of reach. But whatever we do, whatever we envision or plan or go about, we always must take a step forward. And whether small or large, each step requires one key element: self-leadership. If we are incapable of self-leadership, we are at the mercy of those who shape us; we are not the authors of our story but merely actors in somebody else's script. Self-leadership, by contrast, requires an active stance. It requires that we understand ourselves, that we can intentionally influence our beliefs and emotions, and that we can then take the actions appropriate to accomplishing our objectives.

Self-leadership is the beating heart of the growth mindset.

About three years after I bought my first home, I was standing by my bathroom door, cappuccino in hand. Before me was a 1970s-era wood-stained sink vanity; chipped gray floor tiles; and a shower stall that looked like an upright coffin with a squeaky glass door and a rusty showerhead. I cringed at this dismal scene. I contemplated whether to go back to the kitchen and finish my coffee or start a remodel that I knew would require a lot of energy and time.

That day, I decided that if nothing else, I could replace the showerhead. Should be a quick and easy job, I thought, and it will make me feel a bit better about this ugly bathroom. Small baby steps eventually get you there, right?

I put my coffee cup on the vanity, leaned into the "coffin," and reached up to unscrew the showerhead. It was stuck fast. The job was too hard to do by hand. I shuffled to the garage and grabbed a pair of pliers.

As I walked back, it occurred to me that if the plumbing inside the wall was old, it may be rusty and stuck to the showerhead extender. If so, I'd have to use two pliers to do the job: one to hold the showerhead, the other for the extender. Otherwise I'd crack the pipe inside the wall. But my cappuccino was getting cold, so I thought I'd take my chances with one pair of pliers only. I leaned inside the shower stall, squeezed the pipe with my pliers, and turned it.

I heard a crack.

"Porca miseria!" I cursed (along with other Italian expletives that shall remain unrepeated here). Now I'd have to break the tiles to assess the damage. So I took a hammer and started pounding at the four ceramic tiles surrounding the extender. Staring into the hole, I saw that not only was the pipe broken, there were wet rotten studs all around the copper tube.

Good Lord! I had opened Pandora's box (or, in my case, the "coffin's" squeaking door). Now I would have to start remodeling the bathroom. Did I wish I'd started with two pairs of pliers? Of course I did. Who wouldn't? But what I wished even more was that I hadn't waited so long to get started.

I'd had a choice that morning. I could have kept sipping my cappuccino and ignored the hideous bathroom, or I could address something that had been frustrating me for a while. You know what that feels like, right?

We all do: the boxes in the corner of the room, the pile of files on your desk, the "I shoulds" of exercise and eating better, the class you want to take, the issue that needs addressing, and a multitude of tasks that require your attention but keep getting postponed, as if they might mysteriously disappear or somehow become easier.

But these annoyances are not going away on their own. Self-leadership is needed to work on the small and mundane tasks, like my bathroom or your pile of junk, or the more significant life changes and choices, like career, relationships, and self-realization. It's simple, and it's obvious: if you don't train yourself with the small things (your metaphorical showerheads), how will you confront the big tasks and challenges?

The way you do anything is the way you do everything. Showing deliberate, conscious self-leadership in small ways prepares us for bigger challenges.

Needless to say, I could have saved myself a lot of work if I had acted on my bathroom frustration earlier. But at least I was now ready to face the music. In fact, I even got excited. Finally, I could create the space I'd always wanted. I wouldn't just replace what was broken, I would use the opportunity to redesign everything and realize my vision. This was going to be fun!

Most of the best minds I've worked with are the type of people who look at a challenge with a sense of eagerness. With their entrepreneurial minds, they see everything as an opportunity. They don't just think about making "lemonade out of lemons," they enjoy the unexpected, as it makes room for trying something new. Disruption is not a liability but an opening. They don't shy away from reshuffling the cards, they relish it. Self-transformation requires not only self-leadership and a growth mindset; it also requires a capacity and willingness to have fun with it all.

To achieve your goals, you'll need support from people who can honestly hold you accountable for your behavior. I've been lucky to have friends and family who do not hold back from telling me when I've failed to live up to my hopes. My best friends are best friends because they call me on my shit and put me back in line. Such candor is never detrimental to our friendships; quite the contrary, it reinforces them. Outspokenness and honesty are needed to hold yourself accountable and achieve self-transformation.

Lastly, and maybe most importantly, don't go at it lazily or halfheartedly. All too often we sabotage ourselves by not fully committing to the task at hand. Trying to fix a bathroom with a hammer in one hand and a cappuccino in the other is not going to work. It just isn't. How often do we make excuses for why this is not the right time? And we often do so knowing full well that further procrastination will only lead to more rot and rust inside the walls. When it comes to our personal growth and transformation, we need undivided commitment, full attention, and both hands.

The world around you reflects the world inside you. What you think and believe is what you experience. Therefore, to experience something different, you must be willing, even eager, to drop old habits and explore new behaviors. Following the same path will lead to the same destination. Embracing the unfamiliar might mean breaking the pipe, smashing some tiles, and leaning into the discomfort— even if it comes with a series of Italian curses. How could we even think of transforming the world around us without being transformed ourselves?

So let me ask you again: Are you going to die with the music still in you? Or are you at a point where you're ready to grab a hammer and start breaking tiles?

Chapter 19

Play It All Out

It is said that before entering the sea
a river trembles with fear.

She looks back at the path she has traveled,
from the peaks of the mountains,
the long winding road crossing forests and villages.

And in front of her,
she sees an ocean so vast,
that to enter
there seems nothing more than to disappear forever.

But there is no other way.
The river cannot go back.

Nobody can go back.
To go back is impossible in existence.

The river needs to take the risk
of entering the ocean
because only then will fear disappear,
because that's where the river will know
it's not about disappearing into the ocean,
but of becoming the ocean.
—*Khalil Gibran, "Fear"*

It has been over two decades since that day I strutted down Montgomery Street wearing my blue-and-yellow-checkered Italian jacket. When I think back on those awkward and sweaty moments early in my career, I can only shake my head. What a piece of work I was!

So what has become of that socially clumsy guy?

Well, for one, my hunger for personal growth drove me to relentlessly read and learn about subjects related to self-growth and EQ. That was the easy part.

Second, I got what I wished for. The universe kept throwing challenges at me so I could put into practice all I learned. And it worked. I can now say, humbly but confidently, that my life is much more in flow. I no longer get as defensive and protective as that massive angry bull I used to be. I sense with much greater clarity what is happening within me, and I can better anticipate my reactions as well as those of others.

It is much more effortless for me to connect and interact with people, as I understand them with empathy. And when in discomfort, I notice my emotions and the subtle changes in my body. Overall, I feel more balanced and less worried about uncertainties. I am comfortable in socially diverse situations and at ease in exercising influence and creating a space that invites conversations. In short, life has become more pleasant, smoother, and freer.

Don't get me wrong: emotions like anger, disappointment, doubt, and defensiveness continue to appear (as do the occasional Italian swearing tirades). But I manage these emotions with much less stress, and I recenter myself much faster.

Do you ever think about what you would tell your younger self if you could travel back in time?

If I could, I would tell that hot-headed Italian a few things. First, I'd suggest he reconsider his wardrobe, get a haircut, and adjust his cocky attitude. Then, I'd give him a big hug. With a hand on his shoulder, I would tell him not to worry so much, to just relax, and I'd reassure him that everything will be OK. I would also tell him that he will run into difficult people, situations, and challenges in his life that he can learn and grow from, especially if he keeps an open mind.

Winter will pass, I'd tell him, and spring will come; it always does. Have more fun, enjoy life, and take time to notice and appreciate the world with gratitude.

Finally, I'd ask my younger self to read this book.

Obviously, this is not *Star Trek*, and I can't go back in time. Besides, had my younger self read this book, he hopefully wouldn't have made the same mistakes, and so this book might have never come to pass. But my point is this: I wish I had met someone earlier in my life who would have guided me in learning all the elements in this book. I believe it would have made my life not just easier but also richer and more joyful.

We can't look back and change what we went through, but we can decide who we want to be and how we want to move forward from this point on. It is never too late to become what we might have been.

And like the river that flows into the vastness of the ocean, we will never reach a final destination. There is no point where we'll be able to say, "That's it, I'm done, I think I've grown enough." This journey is an ongoing process. Like the river that becomes the ocean, we will only become freer and more expansive.

So, please, I ask you to do just that—play it all out. Keep going, keep growing. You owe it to the world, and to the people around you.

You owe it to yourself to dance away.

Appendix

Coaching Model
Sample Conversations

In the first dialogue, I play a manager who communicates in a direct, straightforward manner. In the second dialogue, I will show how a manager coach might use the coaching framework to engage and inspire.

If you would rather watch the videos for the following dialogues, please go to my website, www.giannicola.com.

FIRST EXAMPLE:
Direct and solution-focused

Manager: Hi, Isabelle. How are you progressing on the application development?

Isabelle: Well, I'm having to resolve a few bugs still. Something is giving me the wrong results.

Manager: OK, just keep at it and let's have this done by the end of the month.

Isabelle: OK, I'll do my best.

If you have worked with people who have a directive managing style, you have probably heard a similar conversation. When Isabelle answered, "OK, I'll do my best," it didn't give much perspective on what was going on, and the manager didn't ask questions to explore what was behind the delays.

By only giving directions and telling people what to do, we curtail their ability to become autonomous and resolve upcoming issues, which will make them dependent on their manager and unlikely to take the initiative.

Now let's have a look at how the conversation would go if we were to implement the coaching framework. Keep in mind that ideally, we want to touch on all five key elements of the coaching model. To make clear when and how these elements are addressed in the conversation, I have noted them in parentheses next to the dialogue. Preferably, you want to move through all five of them in order. Start with understanding the **Purpose**, then move to **Circumstances**, provide **Acknowledgment** as needed, and then help develop **Opportunities** to resolve issues or achieve goals, until you finally guide your coachee into taking

Ownership and accountability. I recommend addressing only one subject (issue or goal) at a time. If, at the beginning of the conversation (in the Purpose phase), you hear several points, try to get them to focus on just one subject by saying, "Looks like you have several points you need to discuss. Which one would you like to start with?" Then come back to the other points as needed and circle them separately through the coaching framework.

Manager: Hi, Isabelle. How are you progressing on the applications development? (*Purpose*)

Isabelle: Well, I'm having to resolve a few bugs still. Something is giving me the wrong results.

Manager: Tell me more. What is happening that is giving you all these bad results? (*Circumstances*)

Isabelle: Well, I have found that parts of the code I worked with were adapted to function only with the prior application.

Manager: OK, and how is this affecting your work? (*Circumstances*)

Isabelle: As is, I'm struggling with it because, on average, each bug takes me about two hours to resolve. Some are faster than others, but I'm feeling the pressure, and delays are building up.

Manager: Quite understandable. You have a deadline and all these bugs can affect your timeline. (*Acknowledgment*) Tell me, what do you believe would be the best way to meet the deadline? (*Opportunities*)

Isabelle: Yeah, thank you, this is really getting to me and adding stress to my day. Let me think. What could we do to still meet the deadline? Well, maybe I can try to run the program on separate servers to speed up the process and also ask someone from the team to help me out.

Manager: Great. What advantages could either of these solutions bring to the issue?

Isabelle: I think that running it on four servers simultaneously could reduce the time to about twenty to thirty minutes each. Then I'll find out much faster what errors come up and can dedicate myself to them while running more code. I think David could also help me out if he is OK with that.

Manager: Great, I'm good with David helping you. What do you need to access the other three servers?

Isabelle: If you can authorize it and submit a request to IT, I'll get it going right away.

Manager: No problem, I'll get on it this morning. Now, before you go, let me ask, what else could possibly stop you from finishing by the deadline? (*Ownership*)

Isabelle: Well, I have to leave by 5:00 p.m. to pick up my son from school every day. He has been acting up lately, needing my attention, and I can't really work much from home.

Manager: Oh, sorry to hear, that must be rough. What can we do to help?

Isabelle: Well, it's possible that David won't have enough time for me and that the servers could be occupied. If that's the case, I'll contact the server department directly and ask for alternative ways to run them. And maybe I'll also include Mary in the process as backup support. That way, if I can't work from home, she could put a few hours in and still keep the project moving.

Manager: This is great, Isabelle. I appreciate the way you take initiative and find solutions to your barriers.

While some of the details of this arrangement are not completely defined yet, do you see how much more Isabelle has been able to share when she has room to develop her solutions? She also revealed something else related to her private life that has been affecting her work. Remember that you need to acknowledge a person's struggles whenever you coach then. Doing so creates trust and comfort.

These conversations can take thirty minutes or they can be short, frequent, and impromptu.

Scheduled or improvised, the format is the same: ask

questions, listen, be curious, and ask more questions to move the client into action.

Offer your support and encourage your reports to reach out to you to discuss progress. As you see them move toward their goals, don't forget to celebrate their achievements, no matter how small. It's a win-win outcome for everyone involved.

SECOND EXAMPLE:
Engaging and Inspiring

In the first example, we saw how you can coach someone to overcome a predicament and develop solutions. What if you wanted the conversation to inspire someone to grow their career or take initiative in their education? What if it were about helping them improve their personal and professional lives?

This coaching conversation could happen in a quarterly review, a one-on-one, or a chat with a friend or family member. Depending on the context, the wording might be different, but the process is the same in that it applies the principles of the coaching model.

First, to guide them, you'll have to get a good read on who they are, what they have accomplished, what engages them, and what they excel at.

Manager: Isabelle, at the beginning of the year you mentioned that you wanted to develop better communication and leadership skills. Tell me, why is that important to you?

Isabelle: Well, my team is growing, and I feel like I need to be better at managing them.

Manager: OK. What strengths do you have, and in what areas do you think you could improve?

Isabelle: I think I'm great at communicating with people and engaging them on a personal level. I can be friendly and easy to connect with. But when it comes to giving directions, I fear I'm not taken seriously, because most of my team has more years of experience than I do. Maybe because I'm younger, they won't respect my ideas.

Manager: I can definitely see how the team connects with you. Tell me more. How true is it that you have less experience?

Isabelle: Well, I tend to think my team has been doing this for a long time, and so they must know better.

Manager: OK, so what could be some reasons they would want to come to you for help?

Isabelle: Hmm, good question. Truly, I think that while they might have many years more experience than me, they are also looking for fresh ideas and new directions. I have shown them how things can sometimes be done differently and that they can benefit from that. I'm innovative and passionate about what I do, and I think they like the energy I bring.

Manager: Great. So, what does that say about your contribution to the team and how you desire better communication?

Isabelle: Well, I think that it has to do with believing in myself and what I have to offer. If I keep that in mind, I will show up with a different attitude and will appear much more confident.

Manager: Absolutely. That's how you'll appear to them.

Isabelle: Yes, I think I'll also *feel* more confident if I remind myself of that.

Through this process, you are making your client aware of their own internal conflicts and you are showing them behavior-changing options.

Now, we can ask Isabelle how she would deal with her growth in the future.

Manager: So, Isabelle, what do you think you can do to overcome these challenges if they appear again?

Isabelle: Well, first, I think I could take a class on building confidence and assertiveness. I know there is one available online in our learning library. Then, I guess I will have to start applying what I learn on a regular basis.

Manager: Great. That would be a good way to get started. Tell me, what would your conversations be like with your team, say, a few months in the future, when you have gained more experience using these skills?

Isabelle: I believe I'll be more assertive and they'll appreciate my input and recognize how much I can contribute to their development, even if I'm much younger. I think this will make me even more connected with them and open more doors and opportunities for the team.

Manager: That would be a fantastic place to be. So, tell me, when will you start making these changes?

Isabelle: I'll look up the information about the online course tomorrow and plan on starting this week. The process of practicing these skills and gaining confidence will take a few months, I'm sure, but I'll stick to it.

Manager: Good to hear that. Tell me, Isabelle, how will you deal with setbacks?

Isabelle: Well, I'm hoping I could talk to you if I'm struggling. I also have a good friend that I've been talking to and he has been very supportive of me. So I'll reach out when necessary.

Manager: Nice. And you are welcome to reach out to me anytime as well.

As you can see, you don't have to be some phenomenal, empathetic genius to coach. Your questions should flow seamlessly and with ease in your dialogue, driven mainly by curiosity.

In my workshops, when I ask people how the questions are working for them, most of them have the same answer: "I find myself thinking about what to ask next in the process" or "I want to make sure I ask the right questions."

If you do that, you are making things too complicated and working too hard. Remember, the key is to let your natural curiosity govern your questions.

By the way, if you feel a conversation is getting sidetracked, you can redirect it with a simple "Hold on. I think we're drifting off-track here. Let's go back to when we were discussing . . ."

Just guide them along. In the beginning, you'll have to remember these steps, but slowly, as you become a better coach, you'll gain experience, and it will all become second nature to you.

Coaching Model
Sample Questions

Here are questions that you can use to become more familiar with the coaching process. With a little practice, it'll become easier and you won't need to remind yourself of these questions.

STEP 1: Establish Purpose

First, you have to mutually define and agree upon the performance goal or outcome. Helpful coaching questions to define performance goals include:

- What are you hoping, as a result of our conversation, to be able to do more of, do less of, or do differently?

- How will you be able to measure success on your performance goal?

- What do you want to focus on?

- What would you like from us today?

- What's going on right now?

- What are you currently experiencing?

- What do you want or need to get out of this conversation?

- How does what you are saying relate to this issue?

- What is this conversation really about?

- I've heard you mention different things—which thing do you want to work on right now?

- What's most important out of everything you are saying?

- How is this issue important?

- What's your role in this issue?

- Where do you feel stuck?

- What is the intent of what you're saying?

STEP 2: Examine Current Circumstances

Ask the coachee to describe their current circumstances. Roll with the resistance; let the solutions emerge. Helpful coaching questions include:

- Can you describe the current situation?
- What realistic barriers exist to successfully complete your goal?
- What are the consequences of this issue for you and for your team?
- What previous experience do you have in trying to change this behavior?
- What is the source of the need to change—is it internal or is it external?
- Where are you now in relation to what you need to achieve?
- What is currently happening that you want to change?
- What other perspectives could there be?
- How would someone else see this situation?
- What do you need to do to shift your perspective?
- What could you not be seeing?
- What is the desired end goal?
- What does success look like?
- What will change bring about?
- What are you hoping to achieve? What impact do you desire?

- Where are you really heading with this? What will it look like when you . . . ?

- If you could set a goal around this, what would it be?

- What is the end result that you are trying to achieve?

- What is the goal of this whole situation?

- Have you experienced anything like this before? What did you do? How did it work out?

STEP 3: Acknowledge

Here are examples for how you can acknowledge what is happening and validate your coachee's emotions. Change the word (*Situation*) for what you heard in the Circumstances part of the coaching dialogue. Change the word (*Feeling*) for what emotion was shared (e.g., tired, angry, frustrated, disappointed, stressed). For example, in the first point below it would be: "Considering the amount of work you are managing (*Situation*), it's no wonder you feel tired and frustrated (*Feeling*).

- Considering (*Situation*) happened, it's no wonder you feel (*Feeling*).

- I hear (*Situation*) happened. That does sound (*Feeling*).

- Anyone would be (*Feeling*) if (*Situation*) happened.

- Nobody can blame you for feeling (*Feeling*).

- It can be very (*Feeling*) when (*Situation*) happens. That's perfectly normal!

- Based on your values, it's no surprise you feel (*Feeling*).

- Well, who wouldn't feel (*Feeling*)?!

- Anyone who experienced (*Situation*) would feel (*Feeling*)!

- Anybody in your shoes would feel (*Feeling*) too!

- Heck yeah, you feel (*Feeling*)! You went through (*Situation*)!

STEP 4: Explore Future Opportunities

Explore what is possible. Allow your coachee to do more of the talking. Elicit "change talk" to increase motivation, confidence, and commitment to the specific behavioral change. Helpful coaching questions to explore Opportunities include:

- What are the positive outcomes for maintaining the behavior change?

- What are the current "driving forces" for changing behavior?

- What advantages will there be for successfully accomplishing your performance goal?

- What final options can we look at?

- Which option seems best right now?

- How can you break that into manageable chunks?

- What are the possibilities, as you see them?

- How do you see the path to where you want to go?

- What are other ways to get there?

- What must happen in order to get that/there/it?
- How can you make this easy?
- How will you move beyond the obstacles?
- If you meet this goal, how will it benefit you, us, our organization?
- What do you need more of: skills, information, resources, support, tools, or motivation?
- What other paths could you take?
- How would someone you admire find his or her way to make this happen?
- What would it look like if you moved more slowly toward your goal?
- Imagine a point in the future where your issue is resolved. How did you get there?

STEP 5: Have them Summarize the Conversation and Take Ownership of the Next Steps

Your final step as a coach is to get commitment to specific actions and explore strategies to avoid relapse. To do this, end the conversation by helping them take accountability for what they are going to do next.

Helpful coaching questions to facilitate the transfer of ownership steps include:

- When are you ready to begin?
- What are the first steps and the next steps you will take?
- What could stop you from continuing the behavioral commitment? How will you overcome this obstacle?

- To whom will you be accountable?
- Where must you start?
- What needs to shift for something different to happen?
- What have you not yet tried that might help?
- What options can we look at?
- How can you break that into manageable chunks?
- How do you see the path you want to take?
- What are other ways to get there?
- What support do you need from your manager, co-workers, family, and friends?
- What information do you need?
- What would someone you admire do in your situation?
- What can you do before the next meeting?
- What are you going to do? Who will do that action?
- By when will you do this?
- What will it look like when it's done?
- How will you know it's done?

References
and Resources

1. Allen, J. (2021). *As a Man Thinketh: A Book That Will Help You to Help Yourself.* Independently published.

2. Berger, G. J. (2019). *Unlocking Leadership Mindtraps: How to Thrive in Complexity* (1st ed.). Stanford Briefs.

3. Brown, B. (2018). *Dare to Lead: Brave Work. Tough Conversations. Whole Hearts.* Random House.

4. Burns, D. D. (1999). *Feeling Good: The New Mood Therapy.* William Morrow.

5. Carnegie, D. (2021). *How to Win Friends and Influence People* (100th ed.). Simon & Schuster.

6. Chamine, S. (2012). *Positive Intelligence: Why Only 20% of Teams and Individuals Achieve Their True Potential and How You Can Achieve Yours* (1st ed.). Greenleaf Book Group Press.

7. Covey, S. (2020). *The 7 Habits of Highly Effective People: Guided Journal (Goals Journal, Self-Improvement Book)* (Anniversary ed.). FranklinCovey.

8. David, S. (2016). *Emotional Agility: Get Unstuck, Embrace Change, and Thrive in Work and Life* (First Edition). Avery.

9. Goleman, D., & Whitener, B. (2005). *Emotional Intelligence, 10th Anniversary Edition*. Random House.

10. Heath, D. (2020). *Upstream: The Quest to Solve Problems Before They Happen* (Illustrated ed.). Avid Reader Press / Simon & Schuster.

11. Lencioni, P. (2002). *The Five Dysfunctions of a Team*. Jossey-Bass.

12. *Man's Search for Meaning by Viktor E. Frankl (1997–12-01)*. (2021). Pocket Books; Revised Updated edition.

www.ingramcontent.com/pod-product-compliance
Lightning Source LLC
Chambersburg PA
CBHW062131040426
42335CB00039B/1947